SEASONS

A Woman's Calling to Ministry

SEASONS
A Woman's Calling to Ministry

by

JoAnn Shade

Salvation Books
The Salvation Army International Headquarters
London, United Kingdom

First published 2007

Copyright © 2007
The General of The Salvation Army

ISBN 978-0-85412-758-0

Cover design by Nathan Sigauke

Published by Salvation Books
The Salvation Army International Headquarters
101 Queen Victoria Street, London EC4P 4EP, United Kingdom

Printed by UK Territory Print & Design Unit

Contents

Foreword

Questions of work/life balance, life-style choices, self-fulfilment and sacrifice are burning issues in today's world, not least in The Salvation Army, which has from its beginnings embraced the cause of women's empowerment. The Salvation Army is not unique in affirming women in ministry and leadership. However, apart from various overseas missions, it is unusual in requiring, in most countries still, that in the case of married people, both spouses must be trained, ordained and appointed. An arena for ministry is guaranteed for married and single alike, counter-balanced by distinct limitations in personal choice. This arrangement brings its own joys, delights, surprises and sometimes tensions and disappointments.

Major JoAnn Shade writes reflectively in her engaging book, not about the Army's history and achievements, well-documented through the years, but a more thoughtful, individual and totally up-to-date account of what it feels like to be called of God, with high and holy thoughts but grounded in the realities of everyday living. Many of the illustrations are drawn from JoAnn's own life, or from the experiences of friends. They will strike a chord in the hearts of others, who will in turn be inspired and encouraged to reflect on their own stories, different or similar as they may be.

JoAnn lives and writes in the United States of America, but she has brothers and sisters in Christ all over the world who will read her book, identify with its themes and thank God again for his calling in their lives and in the lives of others. Like the author, they find affirmation and strength in Scripture, together with the knowledge that feelings, dreams and aspirations are worthy of respect and a hearing in all stages of life, in all cultures – and in all 'seasons'.

Helen Clifton, Commissioner
World President of Women's Ministries
International Headquarters, London

Introduction

I write to you, my sisters, as women whose lives intersect with mine at the point of our call to full-time ministry in the Body of Christ through The Salvation Army. I offer you my own attempt to articulate the themes which challenge our faith and life-decisions as women officers. In doing so I want to validate the tensions inherent in our desire to face these issues in healthy and holy ways, and to offer hope to each of us as we journey through the various seasons of our life and ministry.

The Slinky

Our lives are nourished by images, symbols and metaphor which allow us to make sense of our world and our faith. Consider the toy which in the USA is called a Slinky – a coiled wire which can be made to descend the stairs under the impetus of its own weight.

My son Dan had a school assignment requiring him to create a time-line of his life. The result detailed places and events vital to the life of a pre-teen boy: his first drum lesson, first taste of lobster, first football game. There were neat, measured spaces between events. The time-line was straight as an arrow.

Not so my time-line when I drew it. It started out straight but ended up looking like a misshapen Slinky that had only managed three or four trips down the stairs before it became irretrievably twisted upon itself. That's my story: a sometimes circuitous spiral tempered by cycles which longs to find rest in 'the unforced rhythms of grace' referred to by Jesus in *The Message* translation of Matthew 11:29.

Writer Jan Frank describes it well: 'I believe we're wrong to think our Christian walk is like climbing a ladder, always moving upward. To me it's more like circling along this spiral. We may come around to struggle with a particular issue time and again but we're always going forward, continually being conformed to Christ's image as we move along our cyclical path of faith.'

SEASONS
The metaphor of the seasons provides parameters to the call to grace-filled rhythmic living, suggestive of the words of Solomon in Ecclesiastes: 'To every thing there is a season' (3:1 *Authorised Version*). Cyclical in their patterns but fluid enough to overlap, the changing seasons correspond roughly to periods in our lives, between which we move according to our individual circumstances.

SPRING
Spring, a season of discovery, arrives gradually – at least in my homeland, the USA – in glimpses of red-breasted robins, and purple crocuses peeking their heads through the frostbitten grass, the all-consuming brown of late winter transforming itself into green, fragranced with the heady perfume of magnolia petals.

Gradually, too, comes the awakening in the spirit of the woman as the early eavesdropping on the wooing of the Spirit blossoms into a confident desire to test the waters of the call to ministry. She does not know what this calling will ask of her; she only knows she must – as in C. S. Lewis's Narnia chronicles – walk into the 'wardrobe', push aside the 'fur coats' and step out on an adventure of faith and courage.

What will that future look like? Will she enjoy a solitary walk with Jesus or will her path merge with a man who will share her passion for ministry? What of the coming of children into her life? Will there be enough of her to go around? Young and vital, passionate in her devotion to Christ, one of Sarah's daughters waits, attentive and available for the breezes of spring, the winds of the Spirit of God. Perhaps you are waiting with her. Perhaps 'she' is you.

SUMMER
We yearn for it – the warmth and promised leisure of summer – remembering long, lazy days. We plan for it, feeling the call of the ocean, mountain or woods. And yet its promise can be elusive for the adult woman we have become. At times we wish we could turn the clock back to those days of innocence when a golden summer stretched before us.

Now we face the summertime of our life with ambivalence, knowing its hoped-for utopia may be only a mirage.

The summer of our pilgrimage perhaps brings a measure of adjustment to the man who has become our partner and asks us to stand for our faith in ways that may be uncomfortable or downright tough. Like last year's bathing suit – stretched out, faded or just too tight – we might not fit well in our ministry role at first as we face the 'mosquitoes' and 'sunburn' of repeated exposure to the elements of our surroundings. In the midst of the sunshine and warmth there can come the abrupt summer storm – a daughter's angry outburst, a desperate phone call at 2 am or a son's vacant bed – and our life changes for ever while the days of summer march on.

Yet the sun keeps poking its rays into our hearts, refusing to let us give in. We see our husband in a softer light, God cushions our brittle edges and we glimpse the emerging adult person our child is becoming with a sense of wonder. In spite of ourselves we find strength where we least expect it and rest when we have none of our own. Confusing? Yes, but it is a time to test the ground upon which we stand and find it to be solid.

AUTUMN

Ah, awesome days, those breathtaking autumn hours which arouse thoughts of eternity! Indian summer afternoons surprise us with their warmth just when we were resigned to falling temperatures. Burnished leaves invite us to marvel at their glory. Even as the days shorten, the sunsets kiss the horizon with their 'sailor's delight'.

Autumn is a time to regroup, prepare for the coming months and take stock of who we are. It is a time to move toward the centre, to discard and condense, to integrate what we are doing more closely with who we are becoming. Just as the schools open their doors once again to the young, so the age of autumn opens its gates for the exploration of mid-life.

Autumn days also move us to connect in deeper relationships, through webs that reach farther and grow stronger as we mature in confidence and hope. While the great grizzly bear uses these days to prepare for hibernation, we can use them to soak up the weakening sunshine and prepare for the unpredictable shifting winds of the season to come. It is our Elijah choice: to run and hide or to stand on the mountain in the presence of the Lord who is about to pass by.

The days grow shorter, the cold descends and icy winds blast their way into our being. Winter can be a desolate time of isolation and endless grey skies. Yet the crunch of snow, the taste of steaming hot chocolate, the squeals of children as they toboggan down the hill and the lure of the crackling fire all draw us to the simple pleasures of a crisp winter day.

Winter can bring darkness and death but also light and life. While the gloom of a winter day can be oppressing there is no brighter sun than the one which reflects from the coating of new-fallen snow. Even when darkness descends upon a life well-lived there is a promise awaiting the woman who believes in hope, for God has committed to giving us the treasures of darkness – and to drive us to our knees in search of those treasures.

With the coming of winter comes well-deserved rest, replacing the mantle of responsibility with the mantle of respite from the strain of full-time ministry. It is a time of grace, a lessening of pressure but a widening of possibility for influence that is eternal. While the hope of Heaven grows more real and more urgent, the woman of strength continues to give of her substance – her faith, her heart, her soul. She comes full circle – the one who answered a long-ago call to service awaits a final call: 'Come Home, beloved daughter.'

So enter, daughter of Sarah, sister of Deborah, descendant of Catherine and Evangeline, and find yourself here. As you read, be open to the breath of the Spirit and follow the threads that awaken your heart and your passion.

The early years of life are like the springtime,
Fresh and bright the future claims to be.
Many new adventures beckon,
Many mountains mine to climb,
As the Saviour calls and sets me free.

In the summertime of life I find fulfilment,
Who I am is clear now to my sight.
Each new step is firm and sure,
Choices made are more secure,
As the Son reveals his guiding light.

As the autumn winds of change blow 'round my spirit,
Steadfast in my faith might I be.
May the seeds of hope I've planted
In the lives my life has touched
Yield a harvest for eternity.

Let the days of autumn flow now into winter,
I have naught to fear, I'm not alone,
Wrap me gently in the memories
Of a full and fruitful life,
Until Jesus comes to call me Home.

Guide me through the seasons of my life, Lord,
Make my eyes thy pathway to see.
Through the changing seasons
Let me hold fast to thy Word,
I would walk hand in hand with thee.

One

How Comes the Call?

Ministry means the ongoing attempt to put one's own search for
God, with all the moments of pain and joy, despair and hope,
at the disposal of those who want to join this search but
do not know how.

Henri Nouwen

'GOD is calling me to be a Salvation Army officer.' Words spoken
many years ago, wrestled with last night or whispered in the secret
place where your heart meets God, they are words of massive
implication for self, family, congregation and denomination – and
ultimately for the Kingdom of God.

They are costly words, daring words – words which demand
a response. They resonate with biblical scholar Walter
Brueggerman's desire to find 'a purpose for being in the world that
is related to the purposes of God'. Jean Fleming's image in *The
Homesick Heart* reverberates: 'The call is a silvery shaft of sunlight
bestowed on you through a door slightly ajar, a faint echo of a
conversation originating in eternity.'

It sounds old-fashioned, doesn't it? Who in this day and age
comes to a life-choice by way of a call, a voice straight from
Almighty God? Don't we make career choices based on interests,
aptitude, talent, education and opportunity for advancement,
considering what our financial concerns are – how we can take
care of our family responsibilities while also finding personal
fulfilment? Yet, mysteriously, women are being 'called' to ministry,
to serve God and their community by proclaiming the truth of the

1

gospel and touching lives in substantial ways. In the USA, certainly, women are answering the call, leaving lucrative careers, hopes and dreams and entering Bible colleges and seminaries at an ever-increasing rate.

Within The Salvation Army, women historically have been drawn to officership at a higher rate than men. We speak fondly of George Scott Railton and 'the seven hallelujah lassies' – not lads – who commenced the work of The Salvation Army in the USA. (In recognition of their personhood, the women who came to these shores in 1880 were Alice Coleman, Rachel Evans, Emma Elizabeth Florence Morris, Elizabeth Pearson, Clara Price, Annie Shaw and Emma Westbrook.) This trend has continued through the years, as most training sessions have commissioned and ordained more women than men. That is true today, with 70 per cent of the single cadets in recent sessions in the USA Eastern Territory being female.

AS AN EVENT

I am a 'called' woman – and perhaps you are too, either in full-time ministry or contemplating that choice for the future. For me the call came more than 30 years ago when 'my deep gladness and the world's hunger met' (as the writer Frederick Buechner puts it). I experienced no dramatic voice or burning bush, no coal from the altar or angelic appearance, but I saw a path to ministry which combined my love for Christ with the needs of the poor and disenfranchised. For me that path led to Salvation Army officership.

Commissioner Carolyn Knaggs remembers the days when her husband Jim wanted to enter the officer training programme at a time when she did not sense any explicit call on her life. 'But I promised the Lord that I would stand next to my husband and be faithful,' she says, and together they entered the officers' training school.

Later, during their first year of training, while Carolyn was collecting Christmas donations in the street in Lower Manhattan, New York, she received her own call. The rest of the carollers had gone inside for a break from the weather and she was keeping the bell ringing as people passed by. As she rang the bell, getting angrier by the minute at the circumstances Jim had brought her to, she happened to look behind her and saw a man who was obviously destitute, hungry, hurting and looking more pathetic and lost than anyone she had ever seen. The revelation came to her: 'This is why you're standing here.' She went into the nearby Federal Building and it was there, in the cloakroom, that 'the Lord had all of me'. Twenty-seven years later she says, 'I never took that back.'

AS A DYNAMIC

Like Carolyn, some of us can point to a time or place when we knew for a certainty what God desired or demanded to do in our lives, and we made an obedient (or disobedient) response. But we soon found that the call is not a stagnant, one-time message from Heaven. It is not only an event, it is also an ongoing dynamic, a calling which adjusts to the changing winds of life. Perhaps beginning in naivety or innocence, the ongoing call develops within us.

Spiritual director Carolyn Gratton suggests: 'We have the life process of gradually discovering and expressing that call concretely, in dialogue with the changing appeals discovered in the world as it evokes commitments of time and energy in each person throughout life.'

When we look in this light at the call of God on our lives we begin to understand that it is not just a 'done deal' on the lines of 'I'm called and that's all there is to it'. For me at age 19 there was an innocence to both the call and my response which coloured my early days as an officer. As that call matured it has broadened my understanding of ministry and rocked my convictions to the core. This calling continues to be a dynamic, demanding presence through its continual challenge to me.

Carolyn Gratton explores the dynamic of delight, noting that the call to ministry is unique to who we are, declaring: 'Our commitments of time and energy are evoked by an appraisal of the loving presence of the Mystery in the midst of what needs to be done.'

One person might be motivated by a hunger for justice which involves 'a yearning to help people get what they need and have a right to as human persons'. A second person feels this mystery through 'a deep response to beauty and their intuitive understanding of the way beauty opens the human spirit and refines it'. A third person is drawn to 'uncover the truth of things, for the sake of everyone and because truth attracts them like a magnet'. Still others 'long for a lifework that can express their compassion' because they see that 'goodness and kindness are the face of God'.

It is essential to get in touch with these deeper levels of meaning in the work we are considering. Says Carolyn: 'We need all the vision we can get if we are going to be able to stay with a work through its failures, changes, opaque periods, stress and general messiness.'

The dynamic call is one of delight and wonder but can also be terrible. As a young child in Ohio, noted woman preacher Barbara Brown Taylor experienced this as her deeply respected pastor found himself castigated for his support of civil rights. Barbara writes: 'That was when I began to understand that God's call is not only wonderful but also terrible, that the bright gleam I pursued through the woods and fields behind my house had another dimension I knew nothing about. It had sharp edges to it. It was capable of cutting deep, and those who reach out to grasp it had best be prepared to bleed.'

One caveat: not everyone who chooses involvement with The Salvation Army is called to be an officer. One friend told me, 'I had always wanted to be an officer, but God never called me to that.' As we explore what we are called to do we can also discover what we are *not* called to do.

WOMEN FROM THE WORD: DEBORAH AND JAEL

No biblical narrative directly describes a dramatic call of a woman to ministry such as that of Saul of Tarsus. Miriam, Huldah, Noadiah and Anna are named as prophetesses but there is no record of their call. However, we have the example of Deborah, found in the Book of Judges. A prophetess, married to Lappidoth, she led Israel as a judge – an unusual occurrence for that culture. While her initial call is unknown, she was obedient to the urgings of her people as well as the leading of God. Here is a woman of considerable ability and courage who was willing to consider her calling as dynamic. Called to step outside the typical female role of her culture, she responded to the leading of the Lord even when it challenged everything she knew about being a woman.

The reader first meets Deborah in her role as judge, holding court under the Palm of Deborah. People brought their problems to her and she helped them resolve their differences. Life was working for Deborah, but God had other plans.

Under the oppression of Jabin, a king of Canaan, and Sisera, the commander of his army, the people of Israel cried out to the Lord and he heard them. Deborah's palm was familiar but she was open to the ongoing dynamic of an ever-changing claim on her life. God knew, and told her: 'I have more in store for you, Deborah – will you be obedient to my claim on your life?' Deborah chose obedience, courageously speaking as God directed.

When Deborah and Barak met, as recorded in Judges 4, Deborah spoke clearly of the Lord's commands. She was so confident of the plan she outlined to Barak that when he questioned it she was willing to go with him to lead the army of Israel against Sisera. It was clearly a case of actions speaking louder than words through a woman serious about her response to the call of God.

A BLESSED WOMAN

The rest of the story is a gruesome account that I want to shy away from. I can relate to Deborah for, after all, I am a take-charge woman when I have to be. But then we come to Jael, who was also a woman. She enticed the enemy commander into her tent, lulled him to sleep with a promise of security and then 'drove the peg through his temple into the ground and he died' (Judges 4:21 *TNIV*).

My definition of a godly woman doesn't include ramming a spike through a man's head, even in defence of her people! Yet Scripture tells us that, because of Barak's hesitancy, the honour of eliminating Sisera went to a woman, Jael. 'How blessed of women be Jael ... most blessed of tent-dwelling women' (Judges 5:24 *TNIV*). Although I serve in a Movement which prides itself on its attacks on sin, Jael's story makes me more than a little uncomfortable. But it, too, is an account of obedience asked for and received by God. How ready am I to respond to the call of God?

TWENTY-FIRST CENTURY OBEDIENCE

How do we apply this example to 21st-century women? We begin by recognising that the call of God on our lives is a serious matter, one that demands a great deal from us. Having said that, officership is an attractive way of life which can appeal to some who are not motivated purely by love and sacrifice. A familiar lifestyle which brings fulfilment to our parents or a beloved mentor can be appealing. And when the familial background is chaotic or abusive, the structure and support of the Army fellowship can be a comforting thought. In some countries, too – such as the USA – job insecurity can make the relative security of officership attractive, as can the material comforts of life made possible by the level of allowances. And officership offers a measure of flexibility which many appreciate.

If we are looking for a life of relative ease and material comfort, or power and prestige within a respected organisation, it is possible to find that in The Salvation Army. But if we are truly committed to obedience the time will come when we need to move out from under our 'palm tree' and give what God is asking of us.

WHERE HE LEADS ME ...

In response to a challenge by our divisional commander to consider the 'comfort zone' in which we lived, my husband and I found ourselves asking, 'Are we too comfortable where we are? Is our palm tree too familiar?'

We were serving in a Philadelphia corps with a solid base of believers, well-educated, capable leaders, wonderful music, strong prayer support and an active, effective programme. We loved our ministry, yet God began to disturb and disrupt us. Within days of that challenge we indicated to our divisional commander our willingness to move into inner-city work some time in the future. Our sons were aged eight and five and I was newly pregnant so we anticipated moving in a year or two, giving us time to prepare appropriately for a cross-cultural appointment. But within days of that initial conversation we were appointed to the heart of North Philadelphia, and then reassigned 15 months later to Cleveland Hough, a Salvation Army centre that had risen from the ashes of a civil rights riot in the late 1960s. Our obedience to that call changed the course of our lives, bringing a diversity of experience which continues to stretch and enrich us.

TO FOLLOW

Deborah models for us the essence of obedience to God even when it calls for action which is not culturally accepted or welcomed. It's likely that some men in Barak's army were unhappy at Deborah leading them, and wanted her to know her place. Women may have gathered around the well and gossiped about her husband, poor Lappidoth, having to fend for himself while Deborah was running around with the army, or wondered aloud what she was doing with all those men.

When others in your community fail to understand the passion which drives you to obedience to God, when your commitment to the truth of Christ brings contempt from your postmodern neighbour, and when others in the Army look at you and shake their heads because your obedient response to the Lord is asking you to rock the organisational boat, remember Deborah. Whether under the palm tree or on the battlefield, her obedient response gives us courage.

We must trust that God's plan is right, even when we face opposition. Family resistance, such as a parent being unwilling to let go, or a child who can't face another move, can be devastating. A university professor may ridicule your sense of calling or tell you you're throwing your life away. Even your own will may oppose you, as it whispers that surely you can be just as effective for God as a good mother, a dedicated professional or a committed volunteer in the local corps. Yet against that opposition comes the Word of God: "'For I know the plans I have for you,' declares the Lord, "plans to prosper you and not to harm you, plans to give you hope and a future"' (Jeremiah 29:11 *TNIV*).

COUNTING THE COST

There is a tension between responding wholeheartedly to the call of Christ and counting the cost of that call. Jesus called Peter and Andrew to leave their nets and follow him and they did. But he warned another potential disciple that it was essential for him to count the cost of following. What is the cost for a woman who becomes a Salvation Army officer?

A commitment to ministry makes demands on a family. One is the impact made on the children by the number of moves an officer family makes. A recent study revealed that officer families in the USA Eastern Territory move on average every 3.2 years, which suggests five or six moves by the time a child is 18. Is that something you can accept? A parent's attitude toward relocation can strongly affect the child's reaction, and the stability of the home can provide a great deal to help cope with a move, but it is important to recognise that, even with the current movement towards consultation in regard to appointments, when the orders come to move, the needs of the family must sometimes take a back seat to the needs of the Army.

Another question is: what priority do you feel you must give to your family and how will that affect your commitment to the mission of your work? Canadian officer Major Geoff Ryan raises questions about what he sees as an overemphasis on the priority of family, asking, 'Have we romanticised the idea of the "traditional family" to the point of idolatry?'

Are the priorities of God first, then family, then ministry biblical? Can a first priority to God give us the power and freedom to give flexible priority to family and ministry? These are disturbing questions in an evangelical culture which suggests 'a Christian home should be an oasis far from the maddening throng and godless currents and pressures' (Mary Stewart Van Leeuwen). How do we as women and men, mothers and fathers, balance the 'love at home' image with the war we are called to fight?

A less tangible cost for the postmodern woman is the lack of control and choice inherent in Salvation Army officership. In a culture where there are conceivably no limits for women, officership brings with it many limitations by demanding a regimented lifestyle. A navy-blue wardrobe, a home chosen and decorated by another, no choice in neighbourhood and restrictions on outside work are all part and parcel of officership.

She will be entering what is still largely a male-dominated hierarchical system with its roots in patriarchy and must recognise that, although the Army declares a total commitment to equal opportunity for service, in practice there are limitations on that opportunity.

Can I maintain the essence of who I am in this organisational culture, or will that culture smother and paralyse me? This question can get lost in the excitement of training for officership and in the belief that through our actions we will play a part in winning the world for Jesus. For some women that excitement and belief are enough, but for others the issues of control and choice become a problem as the costs become apparent. While the gospel promises transformation and freedom, the Army's quasi-military structure, patriarchal culture and Wesleyan/holiness roots can lean toward a legalism which values conformity and control. What will it take to be a healthy woman in that structure?

CHANGE

Some women face these questions early on, knowing they are areas of difficulty for them but believing that, in time, the Movement will change. Is this a naive assumption, similar to that of marrying a man and expecting him to change? The Salvation Army is less like a racing yacht which moves swiftly across the sea than a huge tanker which requires time to change course. If we see it as part of our officership role to help the Army effect change we do well to remember Esther, who at danger and cost to herself ultimately changed the destiny of her people. Like her, we must be both obedient to the voice we hear and sensitive in our use of the voice we have.

Given the current climate of change within the Army, as well as our rapidly changing culture, a woman entering officership must consider the effects of changes in what is required of her. What if Deborah had said, 'Lord, I'm OK with sitting under this palm tree. It's something I know, and I can always go home at night. I'm not so sure about going into battle with the troops.' What if Jael had been known for being a wonderful hostess but failed to take the next step God asked of her?

Roles are changing within the Army, and there is a push now to move women, both single and married, into administrative leadership. While many women in headquarters appointments do not want to be confined to women's ministries services but have their gifts and abilities utilised in more-appropriate ways, changes in our structure often demand longer, less-flexible hours, more travel, and greater responsibility. Some of the women filling these appointments struggle with the trade-offs. What of the impact on the family, the spouse, the self?

And what if she changes? In a society such as the West, where it is normal for an individual to have three or four career changes during a working lifetime, what if midlife yearnings bring a new sense of calling which the Army has difficulty accommodating?

An understanding of personal identity can provide support as these costs are considered. Some can say: 'God said it, I believe it and that's all there is to it.' These are individuals who know beyond a shadow of a doubt that the Army is where they belong, and for whom the call to officership is simply the natural progression in their walk of faith. Perhaps that was Deborah's response to God. We don't know enough about her to determine that.

We do know that for Jacob and for Moses, God's call was disruptive. Jacob physically wrestled with God, while Moses took him on in a verbal duel. Even with the tangible signs of an angel and a burning bush, they struggled. Sometimes we must wrestle with a sense of calling that is elusive or confusing.

One woman, no longer an officer, described it like this: 'Once I indicated to the Army that I might be interested in being an officer I felt like a snowball rolling unstoppable downhill. I suddenly had status in the eyes of my corps officers and divisional headquarters, and it felt as though now I really mattered to them. No one ever told me what it would be like to actually be an officer, and after I was commissioned I struggled for two years because I just couldn't do it. It was too much.'

In the end this is ultimately not about us but about what God wants of us. We are called to take up our cross, deny ourselves and follow Christ, and it may be that in God's desire for us to conform to the image of Christ he will require the surrender of certain desires and ambitions.

That's between you and God. He will make clear to you what he wants from you if you faithfully seek his direction. The intent of this chapter is to help a woman consider the many implications of a commitment to Salvation Army officership so that she can respond from a position of awareness, strength and wisdom. As I have talked with women who have left officership, or who struggle deeply with some of these issues, they have often said, 'If only I had known …'

BENEFITS

What of the benefits of officership to a woman? It doesn't sound too spiritual to ask that question, but there certainly are benefits and blessings associated with being a Salvation Army officer. On a trivial level, do you know how much time other women spend each day trying to decide what to wear and what shoes match which outfit? Just think of all the time and anxiety we are spared by having uniforms! More seriously, beyond the material and practical factors already explored, three other aspects of officership should be considered.

The first applies particularly to married women – the opportunity for me to have a shared ministry with my spouse. Now I admit there are days when I wish one of us worked in a factory somewhere, but being able to share ministry is a blessed opportunity. We bring differing gifts to what we do and there is a sense in which our joint ministry multiplies what we are able to give.

Another plus is the flexibility we have as officers. Especially at corps leadership level, a married couple have the ability to decide the scope of each spouse's ministry and how they will share both domestic and officership duties. Timewise there is a flexibility which enables an officer to pick up a sick child from school, or schedule appointments so as not to miss a kindergarten event. There is also the flexibility to utilise gifts within the marriage in ways the couple decide are appropriate. Nearly all appointments can be moulded in a way which reflects the personality and interests of each officer.

A third benefit is the impact for Christ an officer can have. This continues to give my soul fulfilment. In what other profession can you have the opportunity to lead a child to Christ, share in the journey of a family moving from welfare to work, walk with someone from addiction to sobriety, and influence government policy on behalf of the poor and disenfranchised, all in the same week? We have the privilege to weep with those who weep, rejoice with those who rejoice, and give a cup of water in the name of Christ.

When we are willing to risk obedience, God opens amazing doors for us. American writer Annie Dillard challenges us to decide whether we are willing to row out into the darkness of unknown depths or be content with playing card games in the bottom of the boat.

BACK TO OBEDIENCE

In the end, as at the beginning, the bottom line is, can I be obedient to the call of God? If I truly believe God has called me to officership in The Salvation Army can I graciously live with the regulations and whims of the Movement? It's a question that must be settled in our hearts. It can be revisited, but not every time I'm asked to do something I don't want to do or every time something goes wrong. I must recognise that I've agreed to the principles and regulations of the Army and cannot constantly be fighting against them. I must find ways to release frustration and not allow it to restrict the flow of grace and creativity through me.

When it comes to responding to the call of Christ we must enter into our commitment fully recognising what it might cost us. Jesus demands that we love him with all our heart, soul and mind and that requires an intensity of love which evolves from a foundation of truth, not deception. From that position of strength and courage we are able to respond to the call, 'Come, join our Army'.

Two

Alone or Together?

God help the man who won't marry until he finds a perfect woman,
and God help him still more if he finds her.

Benjamin Tillett

ONCE a woman has made the commitment to serve as a Salvation Army officer, she has to decide if she will do so as a single person or as part of a dual-clergy team with her husband. For a single woman, the question which may arise at the very beginning or later as her life progresses is: 'Should I minister as a single person, with the freedom and opportunity that gives me, or should I marry and share the companionship of a husband both at work and at home?' For a woman who is already married when the challenge to officership arises, the question takes a different form: 'Where does my husband stand in regard to officership?'

WOMEN FROM THE WORD: NAOMI AND RUTH
Scripture gives us few examples of women deliberating the choice of a marriage partner, for in both Old and New Testament times decisions about marriage rarely involved the woman. Marriages were arranged and the cultural pressures to marry were seldom resisted. However, Naomi and Ruth each faced a decision of similar magnitude, although initially it involved the relationship between Naomi and her daughter-in-law.

Some marriage ceremonies still incorporate Ruth's response of commitment to Naomi: 'Intreat me not to leave thee, or to return from following after thee: for whither thou goest, I will go; and where thou lodgest, I will lodge: thy people shall be my people, and thy God my God' (Ruth 1:16 *Authorised Version*).

Naomi's story is tragic. Exiled to Moab due to a famine in Bethlehem, Naomi was soon widowed. When we meet her she has lost both her sons, Mahlon and Kilion. Her widowed daughters-in-law, Orpah and Ruth, are with her as they decide what to do next. They begin the journey toward Judah but Naomi encourages them to return to their mother's home. She knew that if they stayed with her they were not likely to marry again, as it was the Jewish custom that a widow should marry her husband's brother, and Naomi had no other sons. Orpah decided to return to her family home but Ruth remained with Naomi and ultimately married Boaz.

Three themes arise from Naomi's story. First, Ruth was loyal to the commitment she made when she married Naomi's son, even though Naomi released her from that pledge. From our 21st-century perspective we may wonder why Ruth didn't follow Orpah's leading, as that seemed more promising than shuffling off to Bethlehem with her mother-in-law, with no guarantees for the future. But whatever her motivation she followed through on her commitment to Naomi.

Secondly, both Naomi and Ruth were willing to face up to the truth. Neither glossed over the extent of their sorrow or pretended they understood what God was doing through it. Naomi returned to her community and stood broken before them, admitting who she was rather than pretending to be something more acceptable.

A third theme is Ruth's courageous willingness to take a risk by trusting her feelings and making an approach to Boaz. What if he rejected her? Would she feel a fool, a shamed woman? What if his intentions toward her were less than honourable and he took sexual advantage of her vulnerability?

COMMITMENT

Can we recognise ourselves in the story of Ruth and Naomi? At the heart of it is the need faithfully to keep the commitments we make, trusting God to work out the details for our good. This differs from

16

a victim mentality where the belief is that 'whatever happens, happens … poor me'. Ruth's commitment to Naomi is well thought through. Ruth was aware of what it would cost her.

HONESTY

A second theme is honesty. This must be a touchstone in our decision-making. If you are incredibly lonely as a single officer and are resentful toward God for calling you to that, admit it. If you are pushing hard to enter officership and your husband doesn't share your passion or interest, don't be dishonest and resort to manipulation to get him to change his mind. Talk honestly about your differences and trust God to open doors of service for you. If you are in a dating relationship with another officer which looks good in public but is troubled in private, be willing to admit the problem before you jump into marriage. A house built on shaky foundations will not stand the test of time.

COURAGE

Like Ruth, when our dreams have been broken and the future looks bleak we can still find the courage to risk and to dream again. It may be the dream will take a totally different form from what you expected, but courage allows us to dream from a place of strength and hope.

NEW WINDS

Had I been writing this chapter a few years ago, the outline would have been simple. As a woman officer there were two choices: remain single or marry another officer. End of discussion. Salvation Army policy did not allow other options. Regulations demanded that both husband and wife must be officers, or neither could be. But in some territories this has changed.

As General John Gowans said when the changes were announced, it continues to be the preference of The Salvation Army that, in a marriage, both spouses become or remain officers. Said the General: 'I consider the Army system of both partners in a marriage being officers to be one of the Army's great strengths. The pattern has served the Army well over many years. I have no intention of dismantling that system. But I also have to recognise that there is no biblical basis for the system, that no other churches make such requirements of their ministers and that not to allow exceptions in some parts of the world would seriously hinder the Army in the fulfilment of its mission. It is that final factor that has been decisive in my mind. I see the concept of officers being married to officers as continuing to be the norm, and the concept of officers being married to non-officers as being the exception.'

However, that 'exception' became possible, in those territories which decided to accept the change. In some territories there is now the possibility – in special circumstances, for it is not automatic – that a husband or wife can serve as an officer while the spouse works in another field and a single officer can marry without being obliged to leave officership.

A WINDOW OF GRACE

These changes provide a window of grace for women who become officers while they are single. No longer will women automatically be forced to choose between their ministry and their desire to have a lifelong companion through marriage. While it will be some time before the results of these changes are seen, it is hoped that by reducing the restrictions on personal choice, especially in regards to marriage, officers will be able to serve more completely and with less resentment toward the organisational structures which bound them in the past.

TOO LATE?

General Gowans admits that the response of officers on this subject, when they were invited to comment, was highly charged emotionally. There are mixed feelings, including among single women. These conflicting thoughts are reflected in the words of one single woman officer who told me: 'There were times in my 20s and 30s when I – as a single woman – truly desired to be a wife and mother, and struggled with whether I should remain an officer. I loved my work, I loved the Lord, but I often wondered if there was a way that I might be married as well. I had a serious relationship with a young man, but I wasn't willing to leave the Army for him, he wasn't willing to join the Army for me (and I didn't want him to do it for me!) and at that time there was no other option. So in the end I said goodbye to him, and continued as an officer. Sometimes, in the loneliness of a sleepless night, I wonder how my life might have been different.'

While playing the 'if only' game is a dangerous one, we must acknowledge its power and be sensitive to those for whom the rules change came too late. Yes, God does provide in other ways, but in the middle of a long, solitary night, what might have been can be very painful.

Colonel Henry Gariepy, writer of the latest volume of Salvation Army history, reports that General Eva Burrows, who was the 13th General of The Salvation Army and unmarried, admitted to him, 'I would naturally have very much enjoyed having children and a family. I really think that was something God required me to give up.'

Does the Almighty ask that of everyone? No. Might he ask that of someone? Yes. Ultimately, the single woman must make her peace with her life choices. That peace may include close friendships, special relationships with nieces, nephews, or godchildren, or outside interests which provide balance and companionship.

NARROWED CHOICE

The woman officer who desires to marry within the Army faces a dilemma. Single women currently outnumber single men by a ratio of six-to-four among those entering training, and nine-to-one after five years of service. For some unmarried women the fear of being a spinster officer is so overwhelming they settle for a marriage partner who is not totally right for them. With so few 'fish' in the officership 'pond' they are happy that they caught one, failing to recognise that their choice might bring both of them considerable pain in the future. Because of the closed culture of officership, once a dating relationship is established it sometimes takes on a momentum that seemingly can't be stopped. It is essential to be aware of this possibility and its potential unhappy results.

If fear is motivating the desire to marry, the single woman must be willing to recognise the danger of this. As Erich Fromm reminds us: 'If I am attached to another person because I cannot stand on my own two feet, he or she may be a life-saver, but the relationship is not one of love.'

Sometimes marriage is idealised by one who has not experienced it. Writes Joshua Lievman: '"And they lived happily ever after" is one of the most tragic sentences in literature. It's tragic because it's a falsehood. It is a myth that has led generations to expect something from marriage that is not possible.' So, just like the call to ministry, the call to marriage must be entered with eyes open.

CULTURE OF MARRIAGE

The other major difficulty for women (and men) who choose to serve as single officers is that Army culture is often biased toward married couples. There are exceptions, but this is still too often reflected in appointments. For example, especially in the early years, single officers are sometimes seen as the most expendable, having fewer ties and responsibilities. This can result in more frequent changes of appointment, often to solve a problem not of their making.

Sometimes, perhaps because of their isolated appointment, the organisation is not geared-up to provide them with the support they need. Or it is assumed that other single officers can provide all the fellowship they need, on the assumption that shared singleness guarantees compatibility.

Over the years I have attended many 'officer family weekends' but cannot remember any such event being offered to single officers. Nor am I aware of any opportunity to discuss the implications of celibacy. With the majority of Salvation Army leaders being married male officers, the needs of single women officers are not always at the forefront of discussion or policy-making.

SAYING 'I DO'

What of those who choose to marry? These women fall into two camps: those who either enter the training programme as a married couple, and those who marry another officer following their training. For those who marry prior to officership, both people may have made the decision for ministry prior to the marriage. In that case, they come together with the same agenda and enter the training programme knowing this is a shared decision. The question becomes more difficult when a couple has been married for a period of time before one or the other develops an interest in full-time ministry. At that point, one may ask the other to follow, the couple may be willing to wait for God to reveal a calling to the less committed spouse, or they may choose not to follow that path at the present time.

The difficulties for people who currently serve as officers may be long-distance courtships or an inability to see beyond the officer role. Sometimes they feel thrust into a marriage that initially seems made in Heaven, but over time just doesn't seem to fit. Within the Army culture, assumptions are made pretty early on as to the intentions of the couple, and sometimes there is the sense that since we're together today, this must be God's will, which may not be a valid – or healthy – assumption.

THEOLOGICAL ISSUES

As a couple begin married life as officers, or enter officership after years of marriage, it is important to consider the theological issues involved in shared ministry. What is the basis for such a ministry? What do you believe about the roles of husband and wife, the question of headship, and how submission and/or mutuality should play out in marriage and ministry? It is a question which receives little attention within Army circles, perhaps due to the pragmatic basis of our ministry, but we must know what we believe in order to have a solid understanding of God's view of marriage and ministry.

SUBMISSION AND HEADSHIP

Early in my marriage I basically 'whited out' the Bible verses which have to do with headship and submission. I didn't hear them taught within Army circles and I pretended they didn't exist, so I didn't have to deal with their implications for my marriage. Passages such as I Corinthians 12:3-16, Ephesians 5:22-33, Colossians 3:18-24 and I Peter 3:1-7 sent a message I didn't want to hear. They seemed to contrast with how I saw Jesus interacting with women, as well as with verses such as Ephesians 5:21 and Galatians 3:28. Yet as I started to look at these texts closely I realised their importance to married people who share in ministry. While I will not attempt to exegete any of these passages in this chapter I encourage you to seek clarity on what they mean to your marriage, and to your work with married couples.

As Christian psychologist Larry Crabb suggests: 'With confidence in the gospel and with a determination to root all our teaching about marriage in the freedom of the gospel, we must be prepared to arrive at an understanding of headship and submission that encourages husbands and wives to sense their responsible liberty to move in whatever directions they deeply desire to move as men and women who are forgiven by God, who rejoice in the uniqueness of their sexuality, who value the uniqueness of their spouses' sexuality, and who passionately long to affirm their mate as a man or woman.'

In our thinking and contemplation of this subject, let's consider how many of these passages are a part of traditional household codes and may have only been stating what was already assumed by those living in the first century AD. It will be helpful to research how the words are used and whether they were actually an expansion of the rights of women from what they had been prior to the coming of Jesus. Does the metaphor make sense to us when we think about what we have seen modelled, both within the Church and within our families of origin? We might consider the question: can a godly woman be both strong and submissive?

Three models may be helpful in our thinking on this subject. The first is based on a hierarchical structure, as advocated by Promise Keepers and Focus on the Family's James Dobson. He suggests that 'women's natural ability to nurture coupled with men's ability to protect, together with women's need for stability and the male ego's need to be in charge, create a complementary relationship where women and men each provide what the other needs'.

A second model recognises that each person is a human being first, and that their gender has only secondary significance. Therefore all distinctions between masculine and feminine are waived. The marriage is egalitarian, with each having equal status.

A third model, that of reciprocal responsibility, is promoted by Paul Lehmann, and described by Duff. It recognises the differences in power, needs, gifts and limitations that exist at various times between a man and a woman. The pattern, however, does not assign power to only one person in the relationship. It recognises that in order for a husband and wife to belong to each other in a humanising context, each individual must have both a centred sense of self as well as the capacity for self-giving. True complementarity recognises that a man's and a woman's need for each other is born out of a sense of wholeness, not brokenness. The need of men and women for one another should not be borne of desperation or the idea that prior to marriage each is only half a person. Rather, belonging and complementarity occur when a centred self encounters another centred self.

Supporters for each of these models are found within Army circles, but it remains the choice of each couple to determine where their hearts – and their theological understanding – lie.

MUTUALITY

Essential to the discussion on submission is the question of mutuality within marriage. Ephesians 5 begins the household code passage with 'submit to one another out of reverence to Christ'. Lewis Smedes speaks of mutuality when he writes in *Caring and Commitment*: 'Committed love is a paradoxical power, because it is a power to surrender. Power? Yes, because sometimes it takes a lot of strength to surrender. But everything depends on what you surrender. Committed love is a power to surrender our right to get what we desire so that the person we love can get what he or she needs. When my desire conflicts with your need, I will opt for your needs – if my love is committed love. Care comes quietly alive when the winds of desire hush, and I hear the whisper of need.'

Michael Mason takes another angle: 'Marriage aims at teaching us that the time we are most ourselves is, paradoxically, when we are busy losing ourselves in another, out of our own depths and drowning in the deep waters of otherness.' He continues: 'Holy matrimony, like other holy orders, was never intended as a comfort station for lazy people. It is a systematic programme of deliberate and thoroughgoing self-sacrifice.'

These writers remind us that the core of marriage is in mutual submission of one to the other, dependent not on gender or status but on our willingness to follow the servant example of Christ.

PRACTICAL IMPLICATIONS

Turning to the more practical issues of officer marriage, the question of working together certainly heads the list. A man might say: 'I love my wife, we share so many common interests and certainly a commitment to ministry, but I can't work with her – she's just too disorganised, too rigid.' This is an issue we might not confront upfront, instead hoping we'll figure it out when we get to our first appointment.

But while there may be headquarters appointments which provide specific assignments for each spouse, the typical corps appointment involves sharing responsibilities and perhaps sharing an office. In our first appointment my husband and I had to share an office, and after six months we erected a wall between us because we just couldn't be that close all day every day. If it's a real problem don't be afraid to ask for a change to roles which are more defined. This could save a marriage which just can't handle the stress of daily shared responsibilities.

ROLE DEFINITION

What about role definition? While there are stereotypical roles for husband and wife they are not set in stone and can be flexible to fit the gifts and interests of the couple. Many find it helpful to define the roles clearly, not just for the sake of the officers but for the staff, congregation and community as well. Some choose to make all decisions based on the individual roles, while others use joint decision-making processes to come to consensus. Remember there is no rule as to how the division of labour is made. Just because the previous officers did it one way doesn't mean you have to.

ENMESHMENT

It is easy for the identities of marriage and officership to become enmeshed and the boundaries entangled. In our confusion we should not be ready to sacrifice our marriage for the sake of the ministry because we are not able to tell where one stopped and the other began.

Saunders, discussing how far the professional relationship harmonises with the marital relationship in clergy-couples, recognises that 'what works in the marriage may not be translatable to the professional situation'. Saunders says two difficulties can arise: 'allowing the games we play as a married couple [to] creep into the vestry and staff room' or finding that 'relating as colleagues becomes the only way you can relate and the marriage relationship wanes and eventually disintegrates'.

The danger is clear: I've known officer couples who have nothing to talk to each other about except the Army and their work, because they have been consumed by the organisational needs and failed to nurture their relationship.

SPACES IN TOGETHERNESS

Henri Nouwen, a profound Roman Catholic voice of the 20th century, speaks to the question of space with these words: 'A mature human intimacy requires a deep and profound respect for the free and empty space that needs to exist within and between partners and that asks for a continuous mutual protection and nurture. Not a fearful clinging, but a free dance. Love is not a clinging to each other in the fear of an oncoming disaster, but an encounter in a freedom that allows for the creation of a new life.'

Each couple needs to work out how much space is necessary and when it is necessary. Because we are together so much during our work, we may need time apart to find that empty space. Since I live in a household of males, we joke that at times the testosterone level gets overwhelming for me, especially during the football season, and I have to get out for a while.

Like so many of these questions, it's one which needs to be discussed by the individual couple, without concern for what other people think. I know officers who thrive on being together while others find an occasional, and agreed, week away from the spouse is therapeutic (absence makes the heart grow fonder).

STRESS

What about handling the stress of ministry, especially ministry together? In a study by Rayburn, Richmond and Rogers (1988), clergy married to clergy had the greatest problems, as indicated in higher scores in stress from Role Ambiguity, Role Overload, Role Insufficiency, and Responsibility. While the opportunities for effective ministry may be multiplied for a couple, it is possible that the stress can also multiply.

Recognising this truth simply takes a realistic view of the situation and allows for intervention. Pressures at home and work seem to take on a life of their own and it is necessary to find ways to relieve some of that stress. It is essential to separate differences of opinion over decisions which need to be made regarding our work from our basic sense of regard and care toward our spouse. It may help to preface a discussion with the statement: 'This has nothing to do with how I feel about you. I simply feel I must disagree with you about this aspect of our work.' And don't forget the basics. Common stress relievers such as a change of scenery, deep breathing, exercise and other ways of self-care are definitely helpful to clergy couples.

SUPPORT

Some officer couples have few stabilising friendships and/or family relationships. A number of years ago, my husband was hospitalised with hepatitis and the doctor wanted him flown to a particular clinic. I felt so alone, not knowing who to call or to ask to be with me or the children. Driving home from the hospital that day, I was given a wonderful promise from God as Babbie Mason sang on the radio, 'I'll be standing in the gap for you. Just remember someone somewhere is praying for you, calling out your name, praying for your strength. I'll be standing in the gap for you.' Later that evening our divisional leaders came to the hospital and I realised that, indeed, I was not alone. However, the terror of abandonment at the time was very real.

There are a number of reasons why officers might feel this isolation and lack of support. In 1989, researchers Kierin and Monro identified these factors as excessive time demands, the need for discretion in establishing friendships within the congregation and the high degree of mobility of the clergy family, which all tend to limit the social support which is important in buffering the impact of absorptiveness.

Just as we can be isolated in our appointments so we are often separated from our families of origin by distance, and sometimes ideology. When the childcare breaks down, we can't call Grandma to take the kids for the day. We are disconnected from the daily relationships available to those who choose to live close to extended family. And when our parents struggle with health issues, our physical distance keeps us from having direct involvement in their care, unless we are able to take them into our homes, and the guilt associated with that inability can add to the pressure of life. Realistically we need to be aware of the importance of relationships, work on them as best we can and not be afraid to ask for what we need from others.

MAKING IT WORK

What are the keys to success for a clergy couple? Writing as a successful clergy couple, Detrick and Detrick suggest the 'key to a successful clergy couple is the quality of the marriage ... depending greatly on two autonomous persons who can relate from personal strength and who, therefore, are interdependent'. One essential is frequent, open communication. How many times misunderstandings about the work or the family have stemmed from poor communication, leading one or other of the couple to say, 'I thought you knew'!

It might be necessary to schedule office time to catch up on dates, plans and commitments, or to make sure you are both on the same page in regards to important decisions. If communication is a problem, Scott Stanley's book *A Lasting Promise* offers effective ways to improve communication between spouses on business and personal levels. Don't assume you know what your spouse thinks or desires. We are not mind-readers, and talking about issues before they become problems is more effective than having to put out fires.

Within officer marriage it is important to find flexibility in adjustment to new roles. This might result from a change in appointment, when new responsibilities are placed on one or both of the spouses. It also can stem from a change within the household, such as the birth of a child, the empty nest or illness on the part of one of the partners. Keep this in mind: it doesn't have to be done the way you've done it before or the way the previous officers did it. There is very little in the 'contract' that can't be renegotiated.

It is also appropriate to discuss and set boundaries in regard to power, control, competition, conflict and issues of gender. You may need to agree on how you will each present yourselves in public situations and how you will handle conflict in your assignment. Is it advisable for you to address differences of opinion in front of employees or soldiers, or do you both desire that to be done in private? How do you present a united front? Will you answer for your spouse or remind the questioner that they will have to talk with your husband or wife, as they are the one handling that particular responsibility? How will you work with other men and women? What boundaries might be necessary in those situations?

The question of time will arise throughout this book during the various seasons in ministry. Married officers must learn to prioritise their time commitments. You're going to be stretched for time. There are disciples to be made and nurtured, spouses to be nurtured, children to be nurtured, your inner springs to be nurtured, your relationship with the Father to be nurtured, and if any one of these is horribly out of balance the rest will suffer as well. Talk about it, make trade-offs, but don't shoot yourself in the foot in the hope of being wonder-woman. It won't work.

Mutual consideration, caring and respect are vital in officer marriage. I want to be able to say my husband knows what it is like to be loved by a godly woman. In this atmosphere of caring and respect we then are able to give each other the freedom to fail. Within our demanding culture there are few places where it is OK to fail, but within a godly marriage we can find ways to offer each other grace. I am committed to respond with grace, rather than sarcasm, ridicule or disdain.

THE PRIVILEGE

Spencer describes a healthy dual clergy marriage in the following way: 'If the scriptural imagery is true: if women express half the image of God; if they are, indeed, gifted by God; if they are, therefore, called by God to God's service; then we mutually complement each other. Together our one flesh becomes a breathing, ministering individual in God's sight ... For the married, self-nurture is spouse-nurture. Together we will all reflect in community the image of our great God.'

The basis of marriage, says Henri Nouwen, 'is not mutual affection, or feelings, or emotions and passions that we associate with love, but a vocation, a being elected to build together a house for God in this world'.

The Salvation Army provides a wonderful opportunity for women to minister, either as a single person or in marriage. With the expanding flexibility of officership there are a number of ways in which women can find fulfilment both in their ministries and in their relationships. Regardless of which choices we make, we have the ability – as Rohr reminds us – to find 'places of sharing where the Word can be shared and where hearts and bread can be broken and passed around'. Might that blessing be ours!

Three

Suffer the Little Children

It was the strongest love she knew,
this mother love, knit up of blood.

Mary Gordon, *Men and Angels*

SHE cradled the two chocolate chip cookies in her hands as her eyes brimmed with tears. 'This is what I have to feed my daughter for supper,' she told me with frustration. At a mandated divisional event, arriving late, missing the refreshments, with sick child in tow, my friend was frazzled. But the details that brought her to that moment of distress aren't as important as the feelings my friend was experiencing: sadness, anger, hurt, guilt, resentment, ambivalence. It's all part of the tension of being an officer and the mother of small children. Been there, done that!

A friend once said to me: 'When I receive a birth announcement or see a bulletin reporting the birth of a child to an officer couple I immediately add that mother to my prayer list, because I believe that the first two or three months of motherhood are some of the most difficult months in the life of a woman officer.'

I remember those early days with an infant in the house, especially with an infant with colic. I expected to be able to continue to do it all, and my husband expected the same. And I tried to do it all, with both hilarious and frustrating results. Far away from my extended family, with a limited number of options for baby-sitting and a demanding first-born, it wasn't easy, but we managed. Then our family of three became four. With the arrival of Andrew, our second child, the dynamics changed again, and

31

once again I grappled with emotions and priorities. Then when our third child, Daniel, came we quickly realised being a family with three children was a whole new ball game!

Just as being a wife and an officer can require a juggling act, the addition of children to the family throws more items into the juggling orbit. The juggling metaphor is useful, implying, as it does that – for a brief time at least – some things must be in the air without the support of the juggler's hands. And when the rhythm falters, the results can be disastrous.

Some parents come to officership with children already in the family, and the children usually aren't sold on the idea of leaving their home, moving to the training school then moving again to an unknown first appointment. Other couples do not have children prior to the training experience and face the questions of whether to have children, when to have them, how many to have and how to coordinate it all.

This chapter will focus on the choices, the transitions and the early years of child-rearing, while chapter seven will explore the issues of PKs (preachers' kids), adolescence and young adulthood.

Biblical examples of mothers are found in the Book of Genesis as well as in the person of Hannah (1 Samuel). Our study of the named mothers in the Old Testament is limited, however, as Esther Fuchs suggests, because: 'None of the biblical mother-figures matches the depth and complexity of father-figures like Abraham, Jacob, Jephthah and David. Only father-figures are shown to experience conflict between, for example, parental love and the exigencies of divine love (Abraham and Jephthah) ... Although motherhood is the most exalted female role in the biblical narrative, the biblical mother-figures attain neither the human nor the literary complexity of their male counterparts.'

WOMEN FROM THE WORD
As we look to these women we will notice that we don't have an example of the tension between rearing children and serving God, because it simply isn't addressed specifically in their narratives.

However, through the stories of Sarah, Rebekah and Hannah the themes of the value of children and the importance of a mother in a child's life are unveiled. Like contemporary women, their lives were complicated, as they experienced blended families (Isaac and Ishmael), infertility (Sarah, Rebekah, Hannah), multiple births and sibling rivalry (Jacob and Esau), parental favouritism (Isaac and Rebekah), and in-law difficulties (Esau's wives, Genesis 26:35).

In Sarah's story, God promised that Abraham would have as many descendants as there are stars. In her desire to see that promise fulfilled, and for Abraham to have an heir, Sarah gave her maidservant Hagar to Abraham so there would be a child from his seed. While she knew the promise was that Abraham would become the father of many nations, Sarah never thought she would bear a son at the age of 90. Yet God defied the biological clock to place Abraham's chosen son in an intact family, born to a husband and wife committed to serving him as the one true God.

When we look at the story of Rebekah we see a woman who also experienced infertility yet who became pregnant with twins after the Lord answered her husband's prayer. A difficult pregnancy was suspected, because the twins were jostling each other, and that was confirmed by the Lord's answer to her inquiry: 'Two nations are in your womb, and two peoples from within you will be separated' (Genesis 25:23 *TNIV*). In Rebekah we see an example of a mother who used deceptive means to further her favourite son's life. She manipulated both her husband Isaac and her sons in ways we would deem unhealthy, but she did so in response to what she believed to be God's direction: 'One people will be stronger than the other, and the older will serve the younger.'

Where is the line between living with integrity, and trying to make God's plan work out? Even without Rebekah's interference, or Sarah's involvement of Hagar, would God's plan still have been accomplished? The question for those women was: could they trust God enough to do what he had promised? Can we?

Hannah's desire for a child, and her subsequent commitment of that child to God, takes us to another level, an extreme of mother-love. In Hannah we see a woman who deals directly with God. Biblical scholar Walter Brueggermann tells us it was Hannah who 'finally dares to pray and to vow, to receive, to yield, to worship'. Her consuming desire for a child (1 Samuel 1) seems contradictory to her willingness for Samuel to be raised in the house of the Lord at Shiloh. Unlike Sarah and Rebekah, Hannah took God at his word and did what she needed to do without the conniving they chose.

These women from history teach us that it is a privilege from God to be chosen as a vessel for the pre-birth formation of children, and for their nurture and development into adulthood. Women have the physical roles of giving birth to children and feeding them, and the emotional and social roles of protecting and teaching them.

These Old Testament mothers also display, in both positive and negative ways, the connection a mother has to her child. The lack of attachment in these stories is puzzling. Where was Sarah when Abraham was willing to sacrifice Isaac? Why did Rebekah decide to be dishonest with her husband in order to further Jacob's chances? Why was Hannah willing to relinquish the child she so desperately prayed for? There is no one model of motherhood in the Scriptures which offers us hope when, faced with similar challenges, we struggle with indecision.

THE GIFT OF CHILDREN

It is essential to recognise Hannah's counsel to us, that children are to be sought after and accepted as a gift from above. Women's studies scholar Bonnie Miller-McLemore cautions: 'Children are not products or private property; children are gifts. About this, Jesus is clear. Nowhere else in Scripture or in mythic literature are children invited in, affectionately embraced, and blessed ... Caring for children is lifted up as a privilege which God entrusted to adults. Adults are temporary but essential intermediaries of divine care, and recipients of an invaluable, irreplaceable charge.'

It is worth adding that children with special needs require special care, and officers with this added responsibility deserve special consideration and support.

THE GIFT OF CALLING

Officer mothers are given two gifts: children and calling. How does the call of God work out in an expanding family? Does the additional role of mother mean the woman must discard the role of officer, or is it simply time for adjustment of schedules, priorities and workloads? Deborah Flagg admits there were times when 'I ... waved the flag of family and children when it was not altogether necessary'. Will there be such times for all officer mothers? Miriam Adeney says, 'To say we can't do it all ... gives us no excuse to drop out of the battle altogether.' What does that mean to my friend who was forced to feed her child with cookies rather than a proper meal?

YES OR NO

Nancy Duff chews on this subject in the context of vocation: 'First, the doctrine of vocation celebrates women's ability to conceive, bear, and nurture children without making it a requirement for achieving "true womanhood".' Women are not required to choose motherhood to fulfil their vocation as women. Women's vocation is not defined biologically. By that I mean we do not have to conceive, bear and nurture children just because we can. Furthermore, because God calls each woman to tasks that fit her gifts, there are many ways to fulfill one's vocation as mother. Each couple must face the following questions. Should we have children? Do we have what it takes to be parents? Can we find ways to be both effective parents and effective officers?

INFERTILITY

Having a child may not be a choice for all women, due to the problems of infertility. That spectre is a painful one, and while we no longer accept the Old Testament understanding of barrenness, guilt and sorrow still trouble the infertile couple. Sometimes medical treatments and adoption are viable alternatives for couples who desire to have children, and there are various resources that can be helpful in understanding that pain, but for those women unable to conceive, the family-oriented culture of the church that defines 'family' as married-with-children can be agonising. Sensitivity is called for, but not always received.

NOW OR NEVER
If the answer to the children question is 'yes', the questions as to when and how many follow. While William and Catherine Booth were champions of a large family, we – unlike them – live in a time when it is generally possible to plan the timing and spacing of our children. But because their biological clocks are ticking, not all officer parents have time to establish their marriage and/or ministry roles before embarking on parenthood, despite the fact that wisdom and experience tell us that the more change that comes at once, the more difficult it is to chart our way through.

WHEN THE CHILDREN ARE ALREADY THERE
When a married couple already have children in their family when they are considering becoming officers, how should they include those children in that decision? How will the changing demands upon the parents be handled within the family setting? Should they attempt to attend the school for officers' training on the traditional residential basis, or should they explore one of the other options sometimes available? These are difficult questions, and open and honest interaction is key to sorting through the options and challenges.

SETTING PRIORITIES
Catherine Booth knew the tension of balancing family and ministry. On the occasion of her daughter Katie's marriage she wrote: 'Mothers will understand ... having experienced the weight of public work for 26 years, also the weight of a large family continually hanging on my heart, having striven very hard to fulfil

the obligation on both sides, and having realised what a very hard struggle it has been, the mother's heart in me has shrunk in some measure from offering her up to the same kind of warfare.'

Yes, Catherine, you are right, and it continues to be a hard struggle, but one made clearer by the setting of intentional priorities to minimise the kind of 'seat-of-the-pants' parenting too many fall into.

Family therapist Brenda Hunter challenges us: 'It's an illusion to think we can cheat our children of our love and presence now and make it up to them later'; and Diane Langberg, a prominent Christian psychologist, reflects: 'I had been in private practice for a short while and it was clear that the practice was about to take off. I had an infant and a three-year-old and God called me (and I know he does not do this for everyone) to make myself of no reputation. I kept the practice open to a minimal degree and sent most of my referrals elsewhere, while I played with Lego [children's building bricks] and Matchbox cars. I loved my work. It was not an easy thing to do. I also struggled with the fact that God had gifted me to do that work and it seemed puzzling that he would ask me to lay down that which he had given. But in that place I learned something of the setting aside of what was a good thing and rightfully mine for the sake of others. In that place I learned that God had indeed called me to do some exceptional things but that he had also called me to learn the lesson of being exceptional in the ordinary – to be holy in small places, loving with little people, unrecognised and unapplauded.'

Yet we cannot ignore our responsibility to our ministry. From the standpoint of integrity, married Salvation Army officers receive allowances on the basis of both partners working. Having flexibility in how we organise our time doesn't absolve us of our responsibilities in that regard. Motherhood is not a pass enabling us to ignore the obligation we have made to ministry, to the Army and to God himself. Miriam Adeney cautions: 'Adapting, fitting in, serving and nurturing are beautiful. We don't want to give up those roles. But we need to balance between being adaptive and being assertive; between serving others' priorities and obeying our own vision.'

SETTING ASIDE

The early years of motherhood and officership may also include a temporary setting aside of certain hopes and dreams, activities and actions. There will be urgent, persistent voices beckoning, but we don't have to answer their enticing siren call. Note that I say 'temporary setting aside'. We do not need necessarily to discard them, but rather to postpone them until circumstances change and make it possible to pick them up again. The tyranny of the urgent should not drive our lives.

What we set aside will vary from woman to woman. Leisurely baths may be replaced by quick showers. The before-children 'extras' – manicures, long telephone calls and colour-coordinated towels folded neatly in the linen cupboard – may have to be stripped down for a while. House-cleaning standards might also need adjustment. While mine drop considerably at times, I recognised early on that if I wanted my home to be open to people I cared about, I had to put aside my pride and open the doors anyway, dust or no dust, clutter or no clutter.

I was freed tremendously as a young mother by reading Karen Burton Mains's *Open Heart, Open Home*, through which I was released from having to vacuum before company came! I'm sure there are times she does that, just as there are times when I do, but she helped me focus on the people who were welcome in my house, rather than its clutter.

This setting aside can also occur in the area of intellectual development. After 10 years of officership, while serving in Philadelphia, I felt the need to challenge myself intellectually, so began looking into graduate programmes. My children were both at school, the ministry was going well and it felt the right time to stretch my mind. But as the brochures began to arrive, a series of circumstances told me 'set it aside for now'. I became pregnant and we changed appointments twice in 15 months, accepting

38

challenging and time-consuming corps leadership situations. Had the graduate programme materialised when I first envisioned it, disaster would have followed. Common sense made me set it aside, even though it initially seemed the right thing to do and there were no guarantees that I could pick it back up in the future. I didn't know if that dream would ever be realised, but I knew it would have been too much at that point in my life. Ten years later, settled in an appointment with supportive staff and flexibility, and a family which had become more self-sufficient, the seminary doors opened and I waltzed through them. It still wasn't problem-free, but the timing was much improved and I was more prepared to receive what God had for me during those two years than I would have been a decade before.

It is true that 'set aside' can be difficult to pick back up, but hold fast to your dreams – children do grow up, much more quickly than you imagine. Not all your dreams have to be realised by the time you're 30.

It's difficult to realise the image of the perfect mother/officer. Mary Guerrera Congo expresses it this way: 'I was repeatedly frustrated in my attempts to "go back to work". I found it required constant reassessment of my priorities. The very ground beneath me seemed to shift and then shift again and again, as I tried to balance my work, my energy, my confidence, my own sense of purpose and direction and of course the child-care needs of my children. What I finally have found is that trying to weave mothering together with work … is an ongoing and nagging and unresolved puzzle in my life … I had not anticipated that grappling with how to parcel myself out among my new responsibilities would finally demand of me a total reassessment of my identity, my talents, my strengths and weaknesses and all of my relationships. I never dreamt that this reassessment would require of me nothing less than the clearest truth about my deepest and most protected feelings and hurts.'

We all know officer families which seem to have got it all together. At least, that's how it appears. The house is always perfect, the mother is an amazing preacher, the kids never talk back and the family sings together during worship in four-part harmony. Oh, that was my cross to bear! Since Larry and I are both musical and our boys have proven to be so too, why couldn't we just get up on the platform on Sunday morning and sing a song for the congregation? We did attempt it once, but after the fiasco of trying to sing 'Welcome to the Family' during Daniel's dedication (with one child pouting, the other trying to hold the baby, both chewing gum, and me wanting to crawl away and hide) I had to let go of that dream!

How glad I am that by the time of my child-rearing years true-to-life television families had replaced the idealised ones of an earlier decade! Life is messy, and expecting to have a perfect family leads to frustration and unrealistic expectations on the children. I'm helped to understand this by the way in which fashion magazines air-brush the photographs of models on their covers. As immaculate as these women are, the magazines still air-brush away the tiniest of imperfections, turning them from beautiful to perfectly beautiful. When we buy into that mindset our marriages need to be perfect, our families need to be perfect, we need to be perfect. It's an expectation that is both culturally-imposed and self-imposed, and it's far from reality. Accepting that our family is what it is frees us to deal with what is true, rather than a sham.

SIMPLIFY

While I've not learned this lesson very well, it definitely helps to simplify. Clutter is like gas – it fills up any available space. If you don't need it, throw it away. Who cares if your mother always baked homemade cookies for Valentine's Day? The bakery makes terrific ones, and apples are even better for you. Place a limit on the number of plants and animals that share your living space. More is not better. The same is true with our use of time. My problem is that I always think I can squeeze in just one more errand, write one more page. The resulting tension when I'm late just isn't worth it.

CARING FOR YOURSELF

Writing in *Families Where Grace is Present*, Jeff VanVondren tells us: 'Your first responsibility as a parent is to take care of yourself. A cared-for parent who knows how to rest in God is a more adequate resource to family members and less likely to resort to control and manipulation.' I myself struggle to accept this counsel, and while I have made some progress, self-care still seems selfish at times. Yet developmental psychologist Carol Gilligan reminds us: 'It is critical that a woman recognises her love of self – that it is legitimate to consider the interests of the self and that each self must claim a certain measure of moral agency.' This seems to contradict the concepts of servant leadership and the denial of self, but sacrifice is only one aspect of mature Christian living. Jesus took time to care for himself (prayer, time alone) and to be cared for by those who travelled with him. When I don't take care of myself I drain myself of any resources I have to share, becoming ineffective in my ministry and mean and miserable in my mothering.

While self-care is important, it is – as my mother would say – easier said than done. When my children were young I counted it a good day if I could take a shower without interruption. But I only had myself to blame if I didn't ask for what I needed from my husband and my growing children. An infant can't be expected to stop crying so his mother can read a book, but it is reasonable for a three-year-old to leaf through his or her own book while you spend time studying the Word or relaxing for a few moments with a novel. Children do grow up and your time will become more your own as they become more independent. At the time it seems as though the baby will cry for ever, but it won't be long before he or she asks for the car keys!

THE SINGLE MOTHER

For the woman raising children on her own the tensions are even higher. She must understand from the beginning of her officership that it takes an exceptional woman to pull it all together. The demands of officership are high enough when they're shared with a partner, but even more daunting when you are alone and also have the responsibility of parenting. So the decision to proceed with officership in such circumstances must be carefully made and thoroughly discussed with leaders.

A belief that God has called you to this work is not enough, there must be a realistic assessment of whether it is an attainable goal, or whether you are setting yourself up to fail. Those who have successfully accomplished this are women who have been able to delegate responsibilities, make flexible arrangements for child care and ask for what they need.

It may be necessary to step aside from this work for a time. An officer acquaintance of mine was widowed while there were still young children in her family and after two years of trying to make it work she realised what was being asked of her was impossible for her to accomplish well. She therefore chose to seek other work for a time. Be realistic, explore your options, negotiate your responsibilities as much as possible, but do not accept the burden of guilt if you are not able to put the pieces together.

CHANGES IN MIDSTREAM
You've got it figured out, life is working, you're finding a sense of balance between family concerns and ministry, then – bingo! – you get farewell orders. Or the pregnancy test is positive. Or some other crisis arises. Now what? Remember that the Chinese symbol for 'crisis' incorporates the elements of both danger and opportunity. Yes, much will change, but change allows us to revisit priorities, learn from the mistakes we made in previous appointments or try new parenting techniques. Changes in midstream can be God's way of getting our attention, of bringing us again to the question of being intentional with our decisions regarding our marriage, family and ministry.

INTENTIONALITY
One of my deepest regrets about parenting is that I took too much of a laissez-faire approach to it: I had a sort of 'what will be, will

be' philosophy of raising children. We never seriously discussed our philosophical approach to parenting, for in our naivety or laziness we assumed that if we truly loved our children (and we didn't define that very well either) they would pick up our values and faith, and life would be good. A more intentional plan would have helped put more structure and consistency into our parenting. There are many good questions. Discipline: who will enforce it? When? How? Will your children sometimes be able to play you off against your spouse, or will you always present a united front? Faith training: will you leave the Christian education of your children to the corps Sunday school teacher or will you have a planned curriculum at home? Who will be responsible and when? What about their education? State school, Christian school, home-schooling? How will you intervene when there are problems? And who will make sure the homework is done, and pack the lunches?

What about emotional and spiritual needs? Will you set aside 'quality' time with the children? Will you have prayers at night, family devotions around the breakfast table? Will you always say grace before meals? And don't forget the teenage years with their issues of peer pressure; after-school work; dating; abstinence from alcohol, smoking and drugs; sex education. While you don't have to decide all these at one sitting, being intentional about how you want to raise your children will pay dividends in the end.

Those are the more practical issues. But there are others. Brenda Hunter asks: 'What do you want your children to remember about you when they're grown and gone? What central message do you wish them to internalise from all the years spent in your presence – the essence of who you were as a mother, what you believed, stood for, sought to give to them? And what do you want them to carry in their heads and hearts? Our children will someday leave our presence with core messages about their worth, whether positive or not. And these messages will influence every important decision they make, as well as their capacity to nurture their children.'

Parenting cannot be left to chance, it must be given at least the same emotional planning and energy we would put into planting a new corps or building a new facility.

THE MOMMY TRACK … OR TRAP?
These questions have left me gasping for breath – and I don't have little ones at home any longer! Sometimes I have resented having to be the main person to worry about my children. While my husband has to answer to his own issues, at times I've been so caught up in what I think God wants me to do for him that I have neglected my children, thereby sinning against them. It may have been the opposite for you – you've been so caught up in what you think God wants you to do for your children that you've neglected the ministry. It happens, probably more than we would like to admit. But unless we are willing to assume God made a mistake in calling us both to ministry and motherhood, we can't totally discard one or the other. It takes hard work, thoughtful pondering and the willingness to risk enough to make mistakes to find the appropriate balance. But it can be done.

MUTUALITY
A final consideration is that of mutuality within a family. As a mother and scholar, Christine Gudorf challenges us that 'all love involves sacrifice and aims at mutuality', while Bonnie Miller-McLemore reminds us: 'The adult both gives and gets, and the child both gives and gets. Children, albeit less adept and seasoned in the practice of mutuality, operate as partners in its temporal dimension and development.' Of course we want to give to our children, but we can receive from them, and not just sloppy kisses and wilted dandelions but also the accomplishment of tasks and the shouldering of age-appropriate responsibilities.

YOU ARE NOT THE ONLY PARENT
A mother in an intact marriage is not the only parent. Officership gives flexibility for both mother and father, and despite cultural

role expectations it truly is the choice of the couple as to how they share their child-rearing responsibilities. After surveying parents from all walks of life George Barna reports: 'By the admission of parents themselves, mothers are at least twice as likely as fathers to bear the sole responsibility for handling each of six key areas of childrearing (caring for health needs, discussing religion, talking about life, disciplining, playing games, teaching values). Only four per cent of the families represented had situations in which the mother and father equally shared the responsibility in each of the six parenting responsibilities.'

Is it likely that those percentages would be substantially different in Salvationist families? Observation would suggest not, but the individual family can be a subject for negotiation. There will always be too much to do and never enough time to do it in the life of Salvation Army officers, so we need gently to negotiate what each partner will do. Miller-McLemore testifies: 'Through many battles, toils and snares, we have haltingly come to a give-and-take that includes transitional moments of self-giving and self-fulfillment for both of us.'

The news gets even better: there is another Parent. My copy of Karen Burton Mains's words is well-worn and tear-stained: 'There is another Parent who perfectly understands the struggle of all the roles you are undertaking – wife, mother, individual – all wrapped into one. His ear is tuned to the young who are mothering the young. He tends his flock like a shepherd. He gathers the lambs in his arms and carries them close to his heart; he gently leads those that have young. So you blew it today as a mother? That happens. You've been acting like a lousy wife? That happens too. You've been too much person and not enough mother? There's a place to go if you want to talk it all out. Let him gather a lamb into his arms. Come on, cuddle up. Be protected. Let the tears spill. Get it all out. Your God is a good listener. Gently he will lead you.'

The best news is that these words do not apply only to mothers with young children in the home. The goodness of God reaches to all of us, in many ways. General Frederick Coutts, speaking to a class at the International College for Officers, said this, regarding our sometimes feeble and frantic efforts to be like Christ: 'Don't be hard on yourself. Be gentle. God understands, hears, and honours the simplest heart-cry. You are his.' Might that assurance be yours today!

Four

Yoked Together: a Study in Contrasts

Our personal differences are numerous enough that they could have torn our marriage to pieces. We strongly believe we have as many reasons for divorce as other marriages that do fall apart, but we have learned to make these differences work for us.

David and Karen Mains

THE phrase 'unevenly yoked' (2 Corinthians 6:14) usually describes couples who do not share the same faith. I am applying the term 'differently yoked' to officer couples who share a common faith but who are not the same. And that applies to just about any married couple I know. Adjusting to our differences – the way we squeeze the toothpaste tube, what we believe about raising children – is a primary task of marriage. These differences can be magnified when we begin to work together in a ministry setting, and can be used in a positive or negative way.

In using the term 'differently yoked' it's helpful to consider the implications of both words. 'Different' can encompass a range of synonyms, including unequal, diverse, incompatible and differentiated. This chapter will focus on exploring how we can be both diverse and differentiated without being incompatible or unequal. In considering the metaphor of a yoke, it is helpful to recognise two things: first, Jesus talked about his yoke being easy, which can help us to see the marriage yoke not as a burden but as a helpful tool; second, a yoke is used to bring animals together for a purpose – to plough a field or pull a cart. Usually, two horses of approximately the same size and strength share the same yoke, so each pulls its weight. In the same way, God uses marriage to bring together two people to share in the purpose of ministry but, unlike the horses, the two 'pullers' are not of the same size, strength or abilities, because the task is much more complex than that of ploughing a field.

God uses marriage partners of different genders, different gifts, different backgrounds and different levels of energy to work for a purpose. In the case of Salvation Army officers, the purpose is the proclamation of the gospel and the meeting of human need in the name of Christ. When it clicks it not only accomplishes those goals but also allows, as Dan Allender and Temper Longman write in *Intimate Allies*, 'our marriages [to] have the opportunity and privilege of being living pictures of the Trinity. We can reveal God by the way we love our spouses.' For some this may be a very natural expression of their personalities, while for others it may be a more arduous journey, but one that must be taken in order to truly reflect the grace of God.

A COUPLE FROM THE WORD: PRISCILLA AND AQUILA

Priscilla and Aquila are a New Testament couple yoked together in ministry. We find them in Acts 18 and 1 Corinthians 16, tentmakers and natives of Pontus. They opened their home to Paul during his visit to Corinth. When he was ready to leave Corinth, Priscilla and Aquila travelled with him to Syria, arriving at Ephesus, where the couple established a home while Paul travelled on. We know Priscilla and Aquila began a house church in Ephesus, because they are mentioned in the final portion of 1 Corinthians 16, sending greetings to the Corinthian Church, their former fellowship.

Our information about Priscilla and Aquila is scanty but we can paint a picture of a couple yoked together in ministry, in comfortable complementarity. Priscilla's involvement was substantial, since she is mentioned each time her husband is, and twice mentioned before her husband, which was not the accepted practice of first-century Judaism. A well-reasoned argument has even been made that Priscilla was the author of the Letter to the

Hebrews (see Ruth Hoppin's *Priscilla's Letter: Finding the Author of the Epistle to the Hebrews*).

Our imagination can help us picture this couple at work in those exciting early days of the Church. They likely spent time being mentored by Paul, and in return provided him with nourishing food, stimulating conversation and a place for needed rest. During one of their long discussions, did Paul casually suggest he would be leaving soon and would like them to travel with him, or was the call to Ephesus more direct or mystical? Did they have a house, a business? Most likely travelling to Ephesus meant a leap of faith. On arrival it's likely that it didn't take long for them to find another home, and to quickly open that home to the people of Ephesus. Perhaps they told Paul, 'You go on ahead to your next stop. We'll stay here and establish the Church in this place.' They did so in a way which exhibited their 'faith in the Lord Jesus and [their] love for all the people' (Ephesians 1:15).

Priscilla and Aquila demonstrated a team ministry, a partnership with responsibilities for each spouse, who blessed each other with their presence. They may have had contrasting personalities but they were yoked together, successfully carrying out the work of the Lord.

WE ARE DIFFERENT

In this biblical example of a shared ministry (the first dual-clergy couple?) we have to wonder: how did they make it work? We considered some ideas in chapter two, but the focus of this chapter is to find sensitive, godly ways to bring two distinct people together, acknowledging the differing characteristics they bring to the relationship and using those differences to glorify God and to serve others. Priscilla and Aquila found a way, and their example gives us hope for our century and our marriages.

At a 20-year reunion for officers I was finally able to articulate how differently-yoked my husband and I are. We were introduced to the Myers-Briggs Type Indicator and each completed a test to determine our type. After 22 years of marriage I knew Larry and I had differences in our personalities but the testing showed we were opposites in all four categories. Extrovert/introvert, sensing/intuitive, thinking/feeling, judging/perceiving – he was one and I was the other. Naming the differences didn't change how we related to others, perceived situations or reacted, but it helped us understand why we respond in different ways, as in, 'Oh, that's your intuitive side coming through.'

Are we the only couple who have these differences in personality? No, not at all! We were encouraged to discover others in the room had similar differences. David and Karen Mains, pastors and writers, describe themselves like this: 'We often think of ourselves as a kind of Christian Laurel and Hardy. "Ho, ho!" God must laugh, "there go the Mainses again – time for some comic relief." Why the laughter? To begin with, we are almost exact opposites. We are well aware that this is not a perfect union. But with God's help it has become a productive union, and we believe that our Lord is honoured at least by our faithful intent to serve him with our whole hearts.'

DIFFERING GIFTS

When two people join together in ministry, whether as a married couple or in a team ministry, they have differing personality traits and differing gifts. Included are the spiritual gifts listed in 1 Corinthians 12-14, but other gifts may be creative gifts (art, music, writing), physical gifts (coordination, endurance, strength), mental gifts (intelligence, concentration, insight) and emotional gifts (intuition, optimism, sympathy). Our first task as a married couple in ministry is to identify our partner's gifts as well as our own, through observation, conversation and even testing. Once these gifts are recognised we can determine how best to use them within ministry, affirming the generous offerings our partner makes.

JEALOUSY

As imperfect people living in an imperfect world, our differences can lead to competition and envy. In listing each spouse's gifts, one list might be longer than the other, or one spouse may have more valued or public gifts than the other. Uneven recognition can result, particularly in the more public avenues of preaching, music or education. When one of the spouses is asked to attend a conference or make a presentation, the nagging voice of insecurity may begin to whine, 'Hey, what about me?' An overshadowed or overlooked spouse can give in to that nagging voice or he or she can accept and appreciate the work of God through their spouse, rather than seeing it as a reflection on their own limitations.

David Mains addresses this subject in his marriage: 'I've learned to make some pretty major adjustments within the past 15 to 20 years. It's taken time because my bias was more deeply ingrained than I first realised. My characteristic first response to Karen's plans was, "If you can manage what you have in mind, sweetheart, fine, but I'm really too busy to help you" – a sort of benign, spousal neglect. I've often wondered if Karen's gifts and contributions to the Kingdom of God might not be more significant, lasting and far-reaching than my own. One of the growing major concerns of my life has been to help complete Karen so she will be all God created her to be.'

Other ministry couples have faced similar questions. Dr James Dobson of Focus on the Family relates the following account: 'When you have a husband whom God has blessed and who is well known for any reason, whether in ministry or business, his wife often suffers from an identity problem. Shirley has been through that. She said to me when she was about 35, "I know very clearly who you are, but I'm not positive who I am." It was an important day when Shirley and I realised that she needed something apart from what we had together. My point is that it's difficult for either spouse when everything focuses on the partner. The other one finds himself or herself saying, "Isn't it wonderful how the Lord is blessing you? I'm glad your talents are being used. But tell me once again, who am I, and where do I fit into God's plan?"'

Mature love chooses to be glad for the other, rather than feel pity for the self, and also understands that public gifts may be ultimately less valuable in Kingdom currency than those quieter gifts of character which God desires in us. It may be a temptation for the 'more talented' spouse to bury his or her talents so the other is not hurt, but that kind of 'protection' disrespects the spouse's ability to be generous, and keeps the spouse from having to face his or her envy or jealousy.

A healthy spirit of competition may spur us on to more effective work, or it can get ugly when one feels put down or disregarded, either by the Army or by the other spouse. Through the years, the question of who is the better preacher has come up in our family from time to time. However, my husband and I have both been put in our place when our kids are the judges, because quality isn't the issue – they vote for the shortest sermon! Faced honestly, the exposure of the sins of envy, jealousy, arrogance and pride will force us to our knees in repentance and lead us to embrace our spouse for the gift of God that they are to us.

VARYING LEVELS OF COMMITMENT
Because of the varying ways a couple can come to a decision for officership there can be varying levels of commitment to both the Movement and the ministry, and that level of commitment can fluctuate through the seasons of life as well. For those who are married prior to the decision for officership, God's call may be more evident to one than to the other. In those situations the 'non-called' spouse may choose to follow the other, either because they cut a deal between them or because they trust God to reveal that to them in time. There have been some who have grudgingly followed, which can cause considerable friction.

In our case I would describe our commitment to the ministry to be at about the same level, but Larry has a stronger loyalty to the Army than I do. What we've come to understand is that sometimes Larry has been unable to see things that should be changed, because 'that's how we do it in the Army', while I've been quick to criticise without taking the time to understand why certain things are done in certain ways. This is usually a good thing. If we were both extremely loyal we wouldn't be able to constructively criticise what we do, and if we were both cynical, we'd be a mess! But until we understood this we struggled when Larry thought I was being disloyal and I thought he was blinded by his devotion to the Army.

THE GENERATION GAP

What I failed to recognise in the early years of our marriage was what I'll call the generation gap – the gap which exists between those raised in the Army, especially those with a long family history of service, and those brand new to its ranks. I'd hear officers say, 'I'm a fourth-generation Salvationist' and I'd think, big deal, so what? I don't think I've ever heard someone say, 'I'm a third-generation Presbyterian.' But, as I quickly found out, heritage matters. Not just in obvious things such as knowing the lingo and having family connections, but also in coming to grips with the impact of the love/hate relationship some Salvationists have with the Army, and in the loyalty others may have because of what the Army has saved them from. Those raised in the Army may not have any conception of the wider Church. Many Salvationists are unfamiliar with liturgical churches, or with other doctrinal ideas beyond the Army, and this can be another way in which differences in background can have an impact on the marriage.

AMBITION

What happens if the couple have different levels of ambition? Perhaps one truly loves corps ministry while the other desires to be in an administrative position, 'moving up the ladder' quickly. One may be a driven type A personality while the other is a less-ambitious type B. A more driven wife may resent her partner's apparent lack of initiative which could be holding her back, or the wife may be angry with her husband's long hours and feel as though he is married to The Salvation Army, not to her. These varying levels of aspirations need to be identified and faced honestly, so appropriate compromises can be made.

A therapist friend told me: 'This is such an issue in ministry couples because what I define as workaholism or sinful ambition in someone working in a secular field can be made to look like holy obedience for someone working in ministry. Who am I to dispute God's direction? Yet when the ministry is consistently chosen over the marriage, the offending spouse is just as sinful as if he or she was emotionally deserting the family for financial gain or career.

SOCIO-ECONOMIC BACKGROUND

Given the various ways in which officers are attracted to Salvation Army ministry (family involvement, introduced as a client, employee, ideological attraction), a husband and wife may come from diverse socio-economic backgrounds. This is particularly evident when an officer marries a client he or she met in their ministry. While it is possible for this relationship to work, a client who has lived on the streets, perhaps addicted to cocaine, brings quite a different background and culture to the marriage than does the middle-class college graduate who is drawn to the Army because of its social services ministry.

While it may be that they can work together successfully, these differences can take their toll in the intimacy of the marriage and in the attempt to work together. Adequate premarital counselling which addresses these potential differences up-front, as well as continued support from leaders and families, can help couples facing these issues. It must be recognised that socio-economic background has an impact on money decisions, discipline issues with children, self-esteem, security needs, communication patterns and many other aspects of marital relationship. True love may conquer all, but people of diverse backgrounds have to work harder at making a success of both their marriage and their working partnership.

CONTRASTING WAYS OF SEEING

We all tend to see the world around us through lenses tinted by our experiences, our background, our genetic make-up and our gender.

One spouse may always see the best in people while the other tends to expect the worst. One may see lots of options while the other focuses in quickly on just one idea. Some of us see the world as predominantly evil while others see it as good. Even our image of God and Satan may not be the same, and that too has an impact on how we minister. Again (this sounds like a well-worn record), awareness of the differences in seeing can be vital in making it work well.

GENDER DIFFERENCES

Larry Crabb asks the questions: 'Does my sexuality merely decorate my soul – or define it? Is there something masculine about men and feminine about women that needs to be expressed in meaningfully different ways as they relate to one another for God's design to be most fully realised in this world?' How does my gender impact my ministry? And what difference does that outlook have on the way I minister with my husband? Simply because I am a woman and see through a woman's eyes and think with a female brain, do I view theological issues in a contrasting way to my husband? Do I have different expectations of people?

Carol Gilligan, writing in *In A Different Voice*, cites studies which show that men view maturity as the ability to separate and to achieve independence and mastery. Women seek maturity that involves forming close relationships which provide warm attachments. Based upon that conclusion, might it be possible that when we begin to consider what spiritual maturity is we look at it differently? A man might see holiness (maturity in Christ) on more of an achievement/mastery level, while a woman might look at the quality of loving within her relationships as an indicator of holiness within herself. Two very different perspectives, but both seemingly reasonable ones.

ENJOYING THE DIFFERENCES

In the light of these differences, what do we do? If we take the words of 1 Corinthians 12 to heart it is good to have differing gifts.

We need the varying parts of the body, male ears and female ears, male hands and female hands, male hearts and female hearts. And we need to understand Paul's assertion that one part of the body is neither more important nor less necessary than another. Our goal must be to utilise all our gifts in sharing the gospel and caring for our people. There are times when someone in our congregation needs my husband to encourage them to get on with taking the necessary next step in their experience, and there are other situations when I am able to help someone revisit past hurts, bringing the Spirit's healing to that pain. Both are gifts, needed at different times.

HONEST ASSESSMENT OF DIFFERENCES

It may be helpful to use some kind of tool to assess our differences, for when we are in the middle of it, it can be difficult to see the wood for the trees. Myers-Briggs is one tool that is eye-opening. Once we are aware of our spouse's temperament we can take steps to work with that in a more realistic way. The Holland 'party' illustration, used in career counselling to ascertain interests, is a good one as well, helping an individual to understand what kinds of interactions they are comfortable with (Realistic, Enterprising, Artistic, Social, Investigative, Conventional). I have also found the enneagram to be helpful in seeing how I relate to others, as well as in understanding my husband's relational tendencies. Once we can see the differences clearly we can determine ways to include our spouse in who we are and how we minister.

COMPENSATING GIFTS

Walker Percy's novel *The Second Coming* features a young female patient (Allie) with a mental disability who meets a man (Will) who has a physical problem which makes him fall down quite often. Since having electroshock treatment, Allie struggles with her memory. As the two fall in love they share the following dialogue:

Will: 'We need each other for different things.'

Allie 'What is the manifestation of the difference?'

Will: 'I fall down from time to time and you are very good at hoisting. It would be pleasant to have you around to give me a hand. By the same token, I remember everything and you forget most things. I'll be your memory.'

By embracing both their weaknesses and strengths, Allie and Will give us a refreshing model for marriage. When we use our differences to compensate for our weaknesses we become an effective tag-team. One can be the enforcer and the other the nurturer. One can be the visionary while the other has the ability to put together the details to achieve the dream. Larry tends to shoot from the hip, quickly sizing up a situation and responding immediately and directly, while I tend to contemplate the various angles, taking my time in responding. There are some situations where his approach is necessary and others where my way of looking at it is more helpful. We continue to support each other as we bring all our offerings into God's Kingdom.

MUTUAL APPRECIATION

Judith Jordan considers the importance of mutual appreciation in relationships: 'Crucial to a mature sense of mutuality is an appreciation of the wholeness of the other person, with a special awareness of the other's subjective experience. Thus the other person is not there merely to take care of one's needs, to become a vessel for one's projections or transferences, or to be the object of discharge of instinctual impulses. Through empathy, and an active interest in the other as a different, complex person, one develops the capacity at first to allow the other's differentness and ultimately to value and encourage those qualities that make that person different and unique.'

PLAYING TO STRENGTHS

Affirming one another is a simple but profound gift and we can choose to be more deliberate in offering that gift. A couple I know has struggled with the stereotypical roles of officers for many years. He has a genuine pastor's heart and ways, while she is gifted in business administration and financial matters. As corps officers they worked for many years outside their giftedness, as he carried the bulk of the administrative role while she did programme and visitation. They knew it wasn't a perfect fit but continued to follow the role models they saw within the ministry. It was only recently that they actually sat down and discussed it. The wife said, 'Why are we doing this in this way? You cringe at having to do budgets, while I would love to trade the visitation in order to supervise our employees. Let's put all the tasks of the ministry on the table and redivide them according to our gifts and abilities. Then, if there are any left, we'll flip a coin!'

They sat down and drafted job descriptions for each other and sent them to the supervising headquarters so the staff there would be aware of the change in responsibilities. Is it working? Yes, and they each feel a freshness of ministry as they have finally found a 'fit'.

PRACTICAL TIPS

Why not try a written job description for each spouse? Some people do well with a natural sharing of responsibilities without ever specifying them out loud, but others find it life-saving to be explicit about what each spouse expects within the work of the ministry. If one feels as if he or she is carrying a heavier load, the couple should try the time management technique of keeping a daily log of what they're doing. The result will be a realistic picture from which to begin discussions.

It's vital as well to address the enmeshment issue. You must find a way to keep business separate from marriage concerns. If you disagree over the style of worship you should engage in at your corps it's possible that the discussion will get heated, as this can be an emotionally charged question. You must find ways to recognise – as one woman officer put it to her husband – 'This is not about you. You're not stupid or ignorant or blind just because we see this in two vastly different ways. It's about the ministry we share, what I think can work, and my personal preferences.'

What you'll find is that it stems from a matter of motivation: you can learn to disagree in a way that blesses your spouse, or you can use the disagreement as a weapon to get back at him for leaving his dirty socks on the floor!

CLEAR COMMUNICATION

Two partners managing a business must have regular meetings and interactions, with agendas and specific questions. Yet often we think we can share the leadership of a ministry without those regular interactions, or we think we can know what the other is thinking through osmosis, because we are with them at home. But it doesn't work. We are trying more and more to have a separation between the corps and home, so I can feel free to say: 'I really don't want to talk about the new shelter proposal tonight, let's schedule time in the office tomorrow to figure that out.'

Communication needs to be clear, and also respectful of the marriage behind the working relationship. Marriage counsellor Everett Worthington's model of identifying the difficulties, not trying to change everything at once, beginning with the positive, analysing situations carefully and not losing sight of the goal (that of communicating valuing love in a positive way) gives good direction.

RENEGOTIATION OF AGREEMENT

Do you have one? Each couple develops an agreement, spoken or unspoken, that makes assumptions about who will fill what role within the marriage, family, and ministry. I handle the doctor's visits for our children, while my husband takes care of the dentist. I oversee the budgets; he goes to public events. The initial, pre-children agreement may be based on an egalitarian concept of division of labour or a more traditional one. Yet when the children arrive, college looms on the horizon, or health issues arise, we can intentionally renegotiate the 'contract'. In dual-clergy marriages, the interactions may become intense and resentment can build when one spouse feels he or she is not getting a fair deal. So put it on the table, come to consensus or flip a coin, but don't leave the issues unresolved.

AT HOME

One of the differing parts in an officer marriage is the sharing of tasks in the home, involving both housework and child-rearing. I reminded my husband very early on in our marriage that we were both used to having a mother who did not work outside the home, and I would not be able to carry the full load of work within the home if I was carrying an equivalent load in the ministry. The result is that most of the tasks within our home no longer have a 'male' or 'female' label, and while some only get done when one of us can no longer stand how grungy the bath is, at least the burden is shared. As both a mother and a scholar, Bonnie Miller-McLemore's observation fits: 'Living in the shadow of resilient rules about roles and tasks, I had to let go of an irrational but insidious guilt because I was not cleaning, cooking, and otherwise ordering the home, and suppress anger when friends and family praised Mark for his "extra" work and told me how "lucky" I was.'

Within Salvation Army culture it may be easier to change role stereotypes surrounding the tasks of ministry than it is for those of child-rearing and housekeeping. I have a brochure titled *Women in the Army* (no date, no author, but probably from the late 1970s), the purpose of which was to encourage women to become officers. It described the role of the corps officer's wife as: 'She is expected to do her fair share as preacher on Sundays, and then go home to serve a cooked dinner which she has left in the oven.'

To be fair, there has been some progress since that was written. For example, no longer do female cadets have to take the class entitled 'Woman officer as hostess' in which I learned that we should never put the ketchup bottle on the table. I've tried to follow that counsel over the years, but those little packets are so hard to rip open with your teeth without splattering that I went back to the ketchup bottle!

Within the Army there appears to be an organisational belief that the major responsibility for caring for the children falls upon the mother (as indicated by the need, in the USA, for only the mother to outline her schedule when requesting childcare expenses), but contrary to that assumption, 97 per cent of respondents in a recent survey on officer marriage indicated that they share childcare within their family. When it comes to the options of working from home, taking the children to the office, and home or group day care, officers seem to find balance in this vital issue within the family. In our case we've both rocked crying babies, alternated taxi-driving and attendance at school events, and found time to offer homework supervision, but we both try to be at the football games – probably because we'd fight over who would stay home!

I've often wished we could have someone in our home who would keep the home fires burning while we are both out working, instead of having to come home at 9 pm to piles of laundry and dust an inch thick. It's not happened yet! But we were fortunate for a number of years to share our home with male college students, and while it did nothing for the housework situation it provided some informal support for my children. While our 21st-century model of family is the nuclear family, it may be helpful to explore involvement in extended family or a more communal way of living with other brothers and sisters, for our mutual benefit.

WHEN IN TROUBLE
When the going gets rough, when the differences become overwhelming, consider Nouwen's words: 'We can only stay together when the "staying power" comes from the One who comes to us. When we know ourselves to be deeply anchored in the divine covenant we can build homes together. Only then can our limited and broken love reflect the unlimited and unbroken love of God.'

Be willing to admit you can't figure it out on your own, and accept help – prayer support of friends, pastoral care, professional counselling. More than 70 per cent of officer couples surveyed reported that they sought help with the marriage at some point, with half of those participating in professional counselling. Marriage in itself is a difficult proposition, and when you add to the marital equation the additional factor of working together daily in a rewarding yet stressful ministry role it's no surprise that we may need help from time to time.

Successful married officership will occur when a couple can figure out what works for them, and just do it. We must be willing to ignore what others think or say. You can also have the freedom to set aside the stereotypes you may have (or that your family has) and utilise the gifts God has given you. It may be that you will end up with a very traditional separation of responsibilities, or perhaps you will not fit the mould at all. The important thing is, it is OK either way. From day one The Salvation Army has been a pragmatic mission – if it works, do it, providing it's ethical, moral and legal. Nowhere is it written that roles must be defined in certain ways. Talk with couples you respect, find out what has worked for them, then build your own model that fits you as a couple.

OFFERING GRACE
Above all, what we do and who we are must be offered in a spirit of grace, both to the people we serve and to our spouses. Because I like to be right, I can barrel right over my husband's heart in order to prove a point. I'm constantly being reminded by the Spirit of God that this is ungraceful behaviour on my part, and I must stop and let go of the need to win. For others, it may take different shapes, but we can each benefit from considering the question: right now, in this situation, am I offering grace to my spouse? Because if we cannot offer grace to the one we know and love most, how can we offer it to a stranger? You know the answer to that, however; it is sometimes easier and less costly to be gracious to a stranger than it is to be gracious to your family or husband.

A wise friend once reminded me: 'No matter what the circumstances, no matter who said what, you have the ability to choose to respond in grace – because of who you are in Christ. You have nothing to prove or defend – that has been accomplished once and for all through Christ's sacrificial death for us. God's grace is sufficient, and covers each of us.'

In the complicated mix of ministry and marriage it is especially necessary to respond with kindness. Karen Mains urges us to recognise that 'vulnerable ego areas need compassionate hands, not the drawn swords of marital fray'. Allender and Longman know this as well: 'Kindness is the gift of mercy. It seeks to transform our spouses by offering them what is undeserved and unexpected.' Doing what is unexpected, especially when it is offered with a generous, gracious spirit, can surprise us with its power for change.

CAN IT WORK?

Rallings and Pratto studied 50 dual-clergy couples and concluded: 'These couples were impressive. They were idealistic yet realistic in their outlook on life, marriage and their work. Undoubtedly they are not "the wave of the future" in the parish ministry but they modelled a satisfying alternative lifestyle for some and showed how an egalitarian marriage could be achieved based on the biblical principle of mutual submission (Ephesians 5:21).'

There are many impressive couples in Salvation Army ministry. They are as different from each other as Alan and Ruth Thompson, a tough cop and a genuine southern belle, who found a very powerful and effective ministry in Salvation Army rehabilitation outreach. Since Alan's death I struggle to think of them separately because when we worked in the same community they seemed intertwined as one. Other couples, either by choice or by appointment, have more defined roles, yet work in complementary ways, each a helpmate to the other.

Smedes knows what is needed: 'What we need most is trust. A commitment reborn each day by our reliable presence, renewed by acts of care, resurrected by generous forgiving. We need to trust each other with our gift.' Allender and Longman describe it another way: 'A successful marriage is one in which two broken and forgiving people stay committed to one another in a sacrificial relationship in the face of life's chaos. True intimacy comes about only when a husband and wife are willing to be broken and to bless one another with forgiveness.' After all, that's how we model the Kingdom of God.

Five

Coming to Voice: the Sacred Desk

We women are called first to be ambassadors of this good news;
we are not called first to aerobics.

Miriam Adenay

ZINZENDORF spoke to the Church regarding the question of women in ministry: 'It is odd when the Holy Spirit says your daughters shall prophesy, and we say they shall not.' The question of a woman's right to preach the gospel has been fundamental to the work of The Salvation Army and to our role as women officers. In these times of changing views of officership, where does this fundamental practice stand? How does it impact what I do on a weekly basis? How do I, as a woman, take my place in the pulpit? And what does that place look like, sound like?

In the USA, married women officers generally preach less often than married men officers. Is preaching an important component of your officership? Oh, I've heard the rationalisations: 'My husband is really the preacher in the family, I just don't have the gift of preaching; the congregation doesn't want to hear me.' That may be true if you're unprepared and only use illustrations about your children, but should any officer be given the option of whether or not she or he wants to preach? Is not the proclamation of the gospel one of the identifying components that defines officership? Imagine your teenager going to a fast-food restaurant for a job and telling them, 'I want a job here, but I don't flip hamburgers!' The manager's response might be: 'OK. Try the pizza parlour down the street.' If the first aim of our mission is to 'preach

65

the gospel' my premise in this chapter is that no officer can decide to cast that aside on a whim. We must continue to be moved by Albert Orsborn's questions:

> O is not the Christ 'midst the crowd of today
>   Whose questioning cries do not cease?
> And will he not show to the hearts that would know
>   The things that belong to their peace?
> But how shall they hear if the preacher forbear
>   Or lack in compassionate zeal?
> Or how shall hearts move with the Master's own love,
>   Without his anointing and seal?
>
> (*SASB* 527)

WOMEN FROM THE WORD

We are hard-pressed to find a biblical example where a woman preached a formal sermon, such as Peter did in the second chapter of Acts. However, the form of the sermon as we recognise it today is a form Jesus himself rarely, if ever used. The 'sermon' on the mount was a collection of sayings, rather than three main heads and a conclusion. So, in the strictest definition of a sermon, we do not have a clear example in the Scriptures for women or men. But when we consider women from the Word and their role in the community of believers we find examples where women spoke to the people, proclaiming the good news of faith.

These women are found in two general categories. The first is that of an icon, one who symbolises a certain characteristic in the mind of the hearer. Women such as Sarah, Deborah and Miriam would be considered icons. They bring to mind courageous women who were faithful in following God, giving leadership to God's people as they were called to do, and speaking when it was necessary.

The second category is that of precedent, in which a biblical woman actually performed the task in question. One often mentioned is Phoebe, an example of a woman who set a precedent when we consider the place of women in the Church in New Testament times. She is introduced to us in Paul's Letter to the Romans, where she is described as a messenger commended by Paul: 'I commend to you our sister Phoebe, a deacon of the church in Cenchrea. I ask you to receive her in the Lord, in a way worthy of his people, and to give her any help she may need from you, for she has been the benefactor of many people, including me' (16:1-2 *TNIV*).

In *The Message*, Peterson paraphrases this as: 'I heartily endorse both her and her work. She's a key representative of the church at Cenchrea.' We don't know enough about her to know whether she preached according to the narrow definition of 'delivering a sermon', but we do know she was considered a deaconness and was of great value to Paul.

While we don't have more information about Phoebe, we have the precedent, the example, of the woman at the well, as related in the fourth chapter of the Gospel of John. Writing in the 1500s, Marie Dentiere asks: 'What preacher [*prescheresse*] has been made greater than the Samaritan woman, who had no shame at all to preach Jesus and his word, confessing him openly before everyone, as soon as she had heard from Jesus that it is necessary to worship God in spirit and truth?'

What do we know about this woman? We first notice that her name hasn't been recorded. My first reaction is, how sad! This woman who made an impact on the course of history is unknown. But so are other biblical women, such as the woman who gave the widow's mite, the woman who touched the hem of Jesus' garment and was healed, and the woman in Simon's house who worshipped Christ in such a tender way. And here is an unknown Samaritan woman who was the one who proclaimed the message of Christ to the Gentiles.

She was a woman who was tremendously changed by her encounter with Jesus. How telling the phrase, 'leaving her water jar, the woman went ...'! She came to the well at midday with a purpose, to get water as inconspicuously as she could. She left with

67

a mission, to tell those in the town what she had seen, and how it had touched her.

This woman did not find it necessary to hide her sin. She was aware of her sin, both in her conversation with Jesus ('I have no husband') and in her report of that conversation to the people in her community ('Come, see a man who told me everything I ever did'). Her sermon very simply spoke from her own experience of Jesus: 'He knows me. Could this be the Christ?'

The Samaritan woman was also courageous and unashamed, willing to speak about what she had seen and heard. Given her trip to the well at midday it was likely that she was a shamed woman, not the most popular in the town. So she took a huge risk in speaking up. Women did not have that luxury in her culture, especially a woman like this one. She knew she had no credibility, but she spoke anyway.

With all this against her – female, shamed, lack of credibility – still she was persuasive. Verse 29 recognises that: 'Many of the Samaritans from that town believed in him because of the woman's testimony.' Wow! I'm reminded of the power of the messages shared in the testimonies of those who have come to Christ through the recovery-based programmes of the Army. While they may be unsophisticated and unpolished, these have an impact that is stirring in their impact. Words that are spoken to the people on behalf of God are powerful no matter the form, and we learn much from these unnamed witnesses, as well as from the feminine icons, the more formal speaking of Peter and Paul, and women such as Phoebe, who very well may have taught and preached in her role of messenger and servant.

OUR HERITAGE

Women preachers have always been a vital part of The Salvation Army. The call to a preaching ministry was one that was becoming more accepted within some evangelical circles in the 19th century, as Hardesty points out. She notes that Finney had a large role in the redefinition of ministry as primarily the salvation of souls, pointing out that such a definition, being 'divorced from intellectual leadership, social authority, sacramental power and moral discipline ... opened the door to women, who were being culturally defined anyway as keepers of religious values.'

Catherine Booth, profoundly influenced by 19th-century evangelist Phoebe Palmer, articulately defined her position, which became the Army's position in *Female Ministry*, published in 1859 (when Catherine was 30 years old). In it she systematically considered the objections, both cultural and biblical, to the preaching of women, and discarded them one by one. The first was that a woman in the pulpit or on the platform was unnatural or immodest. Her response was that 'God has given to woman a graceful form and attitude, winning manners, persuasive speech, and above all a finely-toned emotional nature, all of which appear to us eminent *natural* qualifications for public speaking'.

A second complaint, that a public appearance might lead to inappropriate ambition, was discharged quickly, pointing to the examples of women such as Madame Guyon and Susannah Wesley, which negated that objection.

A third issue Catherine confronted was the belief that preaching goes beyond the accepted role, that there are plenty of opportunities for women to minister outside the pulpit and therefore she does not need to preach. I fear we have moved from the place where this had been a societal voice to where it has become an internal voice – internal to the Army culture and to the individual woman.

WHERE DO WE STAND TODAY?

We as women in the Army cannot afford to discard the distinctive of female preachers. Where are we now, as women within The Salvation Army in the 21st century? In an informal survey of officer-wives serving in corps in the USA, more than 50 per cent reported that they do not preach on an evenly rotating basis with their husbands. Based upon divisional and territorial events, a cursory glance would indicate that the main preachers are men, with the women giving the meditation during the music festival. May I ask why? Are we to assume that officer-wives of our leaders have lost the art of preaching? In an organisation that rightly boasts equal opportunities for both sexes, is there still an argument for more opportunities for female preaching?

Perhaps most telling in our current decade was that no woman officer preached the Word of God during the public sessions of the International Congress in 2000. Yes, we heard the Rev Bernice King (daughter of Dr Martin Luther King Jr) and speaker and writer Joni Erickson Tada, but the inference of that is that our pulpits are open to women, but not our own. Yes, we wanted to hear the then General, John Gowans, for he was the General and he is an articulate, engaging preacher. But was there not one articulate, engaging woman-officer preacher who could have opened the Word that week? I have to believe so.

Are we selling our birthright for a 'mess of pottage' representing lack of scholarship and preparation, of ease, of giving into cultural expectations coming from inside the Army culture rather than from our societal expectations or historical tradition? It's a question we must be willing to face. How ironic that now the right of women to preach has been granted in a growing number of denominations we seem more than willing to abdicate the awesome privilege which was such a vital part of our foundations.

Retired General Paul Rader attributes some of our hesitance to an 'almost paranoid backlash against a radical feminism that threatens to erode the foundations of family and the institution of marriage' and charges The Salvation Army to 'continue to be a standard bearer of gospel promise for all women, continuing to accord them the respect and acceptance our founders sought to guarantee, affording ever-expanding opportunities for women to enrich the life of the Church and enhance its effectiveness'. Commissioner Kay Rader lays down the gauntlet: 'Women must accept the challenge and seize opportunities for making full proof of their ministry.'

SCRIPTURAL CONSIDERATIONS

But isn't there some confusion as to what the Bible teaches about women preaching? Yes, there is some ambiguity in those passages, as can also be argued for the Bible's position on remarriage, sanctification, predestination, end-times, slavery and other issues. What is vital for female officers is that we know what we believe, and that we have a well-thought-through position that we can defend scripturally to others as well as to ourselves.

In her pamphlet, Catherine Booth identified the biblical question as the most serious, but concluded that 'not only is the public ministry of woman unforbidden, but absolutely enjoined by both precept and example in the Word of God'. In her exposition she does as Chaves suggests: 'The solution, hit upon by virtually every commentator, is to make either the first (1 Corinthians 14:33-35 and 1 Timothy 2:11-12) or second (Galatians 3:28, 1 Corinthians 11:4-5, and Acts 2:16-18) set of biblical passages the definitive statement of principle, and then to interpret the other set of passages as somehow of secondary purpose.' Catherine obviously takes the second path, and although the language in her essay may be somewhat dated, her points of discussion are strong, and should be required reading for all Salvation Army officers-to-be.

For a more current and comprehensive treatment of these passages, see *Beyond the Curse: Women Called to Ministry,* by Aida Besancon Spencer, and *I Suffer Not a Woman: Rethinking 1 Timothy 2:11-15 in Light of Ancient Evidence,* by Catherine Clark Kroeger and Richard Clark.

SETTLE IT IN YOUR HEART

Ultimately, each person, male or female, who answers the calling to Salvation Army officership must come to grips with what he or she believes God is calling them to do. Certainly a case can be made – and has been made – for female preachers. It is clearly part of the covenant, the officer-undertaking statement, and the brief of appointment for nearly all positions within the Army, but in the end, it is not about the expectations of the Army or the congregation – it is about faithfulness to the call of God.

However, even when we know where we stand intellectually and biblically, that knowledge doesn't always keep the self-doubt at bay. Leonora Tubbs Tisdale, a seminary professor with much experience in teaching women, states: 'I have been troubled, too, because even the best [female] preachers seem to wrestle with demons of self-doubt … Underneath the self-doubt there seems to lie a pervasive sense, even among women who enjoy and relish the preaching task, that we women are really imposters in the pulpit; that our ways of knowing and communicating the gospel are tolerated as "experimental" … and that our voices, while providing a needed complement to the voice of the male preacher, are still considered just that – occasional complements to normative male voices.'

ROLE MODELS

What of role models? While former Principal of the International College for Officers Colonel Margaret Hay is a delightful exception, having won the award as the *Times* (of London) Preacher of the Year in the United Kingdom in 2000, there is not a large number of active married female preachers in leadership positions within the Army. In the USA, leaders' wives may pray or testify but seldom preach at congresses, camp meetings or officers' councils. In fact we have to reach back many years for consistent role models of female preachers, such as we find in the Booth women and others. They were amazing, those early Salvationist women. Clarence Wiseman, then a captain in Toronto, described Evangeline Booth's effect on her listeners: 'I can remember that when Evangeline rose to speak, there was something like an electric shock through the crowd. She commanded that audience. There was a certain charisma about her, and we were electrified by her message.'

One of the reasons my pulpit ministry has priority for me is its importance to future generations, just as that of Catherine's laid the foundation for my ministry. I want my sons to know that women can open the Word of God. I want the young women in my congregation to know that they too can be preachers one day.

IN A DIFFERENT VOICE

In a Different Voice by Carol Gilligan has become a prominent work in the development of a psychology of women. The author believes the psychological establishment made certain judgments as to what appeared to be mental illness based upon studies of men and then carried those assumptions into their work with women. Gilligan's premise is that women do relate to the world around them in a way that is different from men, but that 'different' is not necessarily 'less than' or aberrant. The same is true in the pulpit. 'Different' does not equal 'inferior' or 'less effective'.

Carol Noren, writing in *The Woman in the Pulpit*, points out: 'We live in a curious era of Church history, when talking about the distinctive gifts and liabilities that women bring to pulpit ministry can mean risking accusation of sexism on the one hand or strident feminism on the other. And yet both clergy and laity can benefit from an examination of what happens when the voice proclaiming the Word is feminine.'

Linguistically, women as a whole speak with a different voice from men. Linguist Robin Lakoff showed in groundbreaking research carried out in America in 1975 that there are speech patterns which are used more by women than men and that as a result women are in a double bind: 'If they speak as they have been trained to speak – like "ladies" – then they are considered by men to be weak, subservient, and ineffectual. If they adopt the language patterns of men, however, they are deemed to be aggressive, domineering, and pushy.'

The patterns of speech associated with women include the more frequent use of questions, the use of the intensive 'so' more often, and hypercorrect grammar. Perhaps most important to the subject of preaching, they more commonly use 'provisional speech, which uses qualifiers (some, most, many), hedges (perhaps, I think), and tag questions (this is an important truth, isn't it?). These patterns can be helpful in our preaching, or can become problematic.

Our different voice is not only found in our use of linguistic patterns, but also in the way this voice addresses biblical topics. Elaine J. Lawless notes that women's sermons historically are 'about connection and dialogue, about inclusion and broadening perspectives. Their messages are of restoration and healing'. This different voice becomes an important voice if a full picture of the gospel message is desired.

It's possible to use our different voice to make an impact on those listening to our teaching and preaching. We don't have to preach like men! I could never in a million years preach as loudly or as dynamically as my husband, but 'a soft word ...'. I may not be comfortable using a military analogy but I can use illustrations from my reading, my hobbies and, yes, even children's television programmes. One of my favourite illustrations is a children's song that talks about a cookie crumbling if it's held too tightly. It is an easily understood illustration of buried treasure, unused talents and hoarded resources, illustrating Jesus' words, 'If you grasp and cling to life on your own terms, you'll lose it, but if you let that life go, you'll get life on God's terms' (Luke 17 *The Message*)

Beyond the use of situational illustrations, it is a voice that can also speak from a woman's understanding of creation, childbirth, care-giving and relationship. Barbara Brown Taylor does it very naturally. In preparing to preach from John 6 (feeding of the multitudes, bread of heaven) she uses these words: 'While I was mulling it all over, I spent some time with my new goddaughter, Madeline. Just three months old, she lived in her mother's arms, comforted by the familiar sounds and smells of the one-person universe into which she had been born. She slept, she woke, she fed at her mother's breast, finding everything she needed in that one nourishing embrace. Watching her ... I saw that her mother was truly her food, the body and blood from which her own flesh had been made and from which she daily accepted her life as a matter of course.'

FROM WHERE YOU'RE AT

It is appropriate to preach from where you're at. If you were up all night with a crying baby and are hopelessly exhausted, you can describe how Jesus felt when pursued by the needs of the crowd. Jesus used simple lessons from simple items – seeds, lost coins, water jugs, wayward sons – to teach eternal concepts, and we can do the same. I still remember a sermon my friend Major Lauren Hodgson preached a number of years ago on a Sunday night at our corps. She painted a vivid picture by describing her return home from overseas service with a baby and a toddler, car seats, strollers and luggage – and what a tremendous relief it was to finally be able to put those 'burdens' down. My arms actually ached as she finished her description, and she had me hooked as she began to speak of how much our Heavenly Father wants us to lay our burdens at his feet so he can pick them up and carry them for us.

Catherine Booth wrote of what it was like to be a young mother called to preach: 'If I had only time to study and write I should not fear now, but I must be content to do what I can consistently with my home duties and leave the future to the Lord.' Her example of commitment to a preaching ministry is illustrated in the description of meetings in London's St John's Wood: 'To these congregations (more than three parts, it is recorded, were men) she poured out her thoughts, reasoned, denounced, pleaded. Mrs Booth set forth God's truth without passion or eccentricity but with profound earnestness and was to multitudes of educated people like a messenger from God.'

Those meetings were concluded towards the end of March, and on 28 April 1868 her eighth child, Lucy Milward, was born!

As Catherine would be quick to remind us, we must not use our personal circumstances as an excuse to preach only from where we are, even if knee-deep in nappies. Preaching should stretch the preacher, both in preparation and delivery, much more than it does the listener. What are you currently reading to aid your preaching ministry? What are you listening to, how are you broadening your understanding of theological concepts, who are you talking with to discuss hard topics?

SELF-DISCLOSURE

Often the question is raised, how much self-disclosure is appropriate? A woman may be more likely to speak of her own heart struggles, and that can be a legitimate part of your preaching, but do it with caution. Once it is said, it can't be taken back, so we must strive to find a balance between transparency and appropriate self-protection, especially when it involves others in our family. A good rule of thumb is to ask permission before you use stories about your children or husband which reveal anything that reflects on them personally. Don't always make yourself or your family the heroes either. We must also take care not to work out our own therapy from the pulpit. Catharsis and confession have their place within a caring community of believers, but not generally from the pulpit.

Professor of Homiletics at Yale Divinity School Leonara Tubbs Tisdale encourages us: 'Through the telling of their own stories, women model for the community of faith how to find, in the ordinary, mundane experiences of everyday life, inbreakings of the holy. Through the telling of their own stories, women keep the gospel close to the ground, making very local connections between the biblical story and our lived lives. Through the telling of their own stories, women provide an accessible model through which children and less educated folk in a congregation can find their own voices and give expression to their own faith and understanding. Through the telling of their own authentic stories, women provide a needed corrective to a pulpit too long held hostage by sports stories, war stories and canned illustrations of every variety.'

MAKING IT WORK

What are some of the practical issues female preachers must face? We can begin by taking advantage of the resources women bring to the pulpit. Women are well-equipped to use imagery in powerful ways in their preaching. Jesus often used metaphors, and they can be quite effective in awakening hunger for God. In the use of metaphor and imagery, consider how you can speak to all five senses. Certain smells and tastes evoke particular memories or reactions. For instance, sin can be modified by the word bitter, or it can be described as leaving the taste of a melted aspirin on your tongue. Help your listeners to do more than hear the word – help them to see it, taste it, smell it and touch it.

Consider how Barbara Brown Taylor does it in these two examples: '[Jesus' words] brought the Pharisees charging after him like a bull in a china shop.' 'When God's gifts come wrapped in shiny paper and curled ribbon, we say "thank you very much" but when they arrive on our doorstep held together with newspapers and barbed wire, most of us take out our magic markers and write "Return to Sender" on the box.'

Understand the linguistic differences and take advantage of them. Help your congregation to know that they can wrestle with the text. The hedges and qualifiers can be an invitation to further thought and study, rather than a dogmatic acceptance of the preacher's interpretation. These forms can also open the door to further dialogue and to a sense of including the congregation in that dialogue. Draw them in, rather than simply tell them the way it is.

Use your feminine wiles. There I go, crossing the lines of political incorrectness. But don't forget – if preaching is only exposition, we've failed. It must also be persuasion – and women can be persuasive. As we read accounts of the early women preachers in the Army this appears to be an important part of their preaching. Catherine Booth was described in these words: 'Her real eloquence, with all its quaint and even grotesque forms of pronunciation and grammar ... is a powerful engine of persuasion; but she possesses more than mere rhetoric, however varied and vivifying. She has an immense store of sound sense and practical experience, combined with a genuinely high ideal of life and duty.'

FILTERS

Think about how you are heard when you preach. We all have filters through which we hear another, and it is beneficial to the preacher to be aware of this. Noren says: 'Rather than merely being frustrated by cultural filters through which people listen to a woman preacher, I can begin to anticipate those filters, and choose to work with them, work around them, or challenge them head on.' Consider what cultural filters there may be: some may hear a woman through the voice of their mother, scolding or always finding fault, or speaking to her little prince or princess. Other filters may be those of poor relationships with women, a fight with their wife on the way to the meeting, or involvement with pornography that taints any message coming from a woman. Obviously, we cannot know what each person's filters may be, but it is useful to our preparation to keep those potential filters in mind.

FEEDBACK

One of the most effective ways to improve your preaching is to be brave enough to ask for honest feedback. It may be that you will initially want to ask for that from one or two trusted members of the congregation, explaining that you are motivated to ask by a desire to improve your ability to communicate the gospel. If you want to risk more, you may want to ask a few of the teens to meet with you to discuss your sermon, or ask them to take notes and share them with you. There's nothing like the perspective of a teenager to open your eyes to how you're seen by others.

While I was doing my internship in counselling during my time in seminary, I initially dreaded having to present a case in supervision, not wanting to hear myself or watch the videotape, and afraid of critical feedback. However, I soon learned to appreciate getting reaction on how I was received because self-evaluation can be difficult. I found that my supervisors wanted me to learn to be an effective therapist and had much to offer me in the way of constructive criticism and positive encouragement. The same could be true of at least a few members of your congregation.

YOUR OWN VOICE

Don't be afraid to develop your own style of preaching. You don't have to be a clone of anyone else. If you're a bubbly, enthusiastic woman you don't have to become sombre in the pulpit. If you are a reflective, deep thinker, gimmicks may not be your thing, so don't give in to the temptation to think you have to do that simply because someone else does it so well. Think about your preaching, about what has felt comfortable and what hasn't gelled, and go with your strengths as you discover your own expression of faith and witness.

A successful female preacher is not afraid to use her face. I'm so glad I no longer have to wear a hat on the platform. I always felt that was a barrier to connecting with the congregation. I know we can send messages with our eyes, on a continuum from tender, empathic compassion to vile hatred. So let your eyes work for you, not just to make a point but also to observe the impact your words are having.

FINDING ROLE MODELS

We can be both encouraged and challenged by reading sermons by women, historical and current. Try to put aside the differences in the use of language that keep us from connecting with Catherine and Evangeline Booth's sermons, and perhaps even try to rewrite one of them in contemporary idiom. Look for what makes sermons by women different from those written by men. Listen for the heart of a woman through her words. Ask yourself the questions: When I finished reading this sermon, did I know who this woman was? Did I have a better sense of who God is and what he wants of me? Be aware of her use of imagery, of story, of truth. As an example, Lauren Artress says: 'The Christian tradition divides sins into two categories – warm and cold. We pay a great deal of attention to warm sins, sins of the flesh, and we ignore the cold sins, sins of the hardened heart.' What is different about the way she describes this idea? In exploring the warm/cold dichotomy further, how might a woman's view be different from a man's view?

When you hear a woman preach, do so with a critical ear and eye. Notice how she uses her voice, her face, her body. Consider how she influences you as she speaks. What is your reaction to her voice, her gestures? Does the content feed your soul? Allow yourself also to respond emotionally to her message. Can you connect with her as a person as she speaks? How is God speaking to you through her? As you see and hear her, how does that help you to see yourself?

DON'TS

There are a few 'don'ts' we need to be reminded of. The first is, don't whine. Most likely, your listeners face the same kinds of circumstances as you but with fewer resources to meet them. We have the awesome responsibility to offer hope, not add to discouragement. I'm not suggesting we should put on a mask when we step into the pulpit, because our voice must be authentic, but we must do all we can do to lift Jesus up as we proclaim the good news of the gospel.

Don't placate. Life is difficult, and while we know that God is both good and powerful there is no need to turn him into a fairy-tale God who will make everyone live happily ever after. Speak the truth in love. Also, don't dumb down your message. While it is essential to communicate in ways our listeners understand, we must encourage them to grow up in their faith by offering them the meat of the gospel as well as the milk. Look at each sermon with an eye to whether it has something in it that can be comprehended by the newest babe in Christ while also offering something of substance to the one who desires to go deeper. Don't always preach to the lowest common denominator.

Commissioner Kay Rader, wife of Retired General Paul Rader, speaking in officers' councils on the subject of women preachers, warned of two things in regard to our preaching. The first was, 'Don't go over time.' Remember a present-day Eutychus may be sitting on the window sill (see Acts 20:9). While Catherine Booth was able to preach effectively for more than an hour, we are preaching to people who are used to television programmes with three-minute segments. That doesn't mean we have to keep our messages to three minutes or focus on entertaining the people, but we should be aware of whether we are holding the attention of the majority of the congregation. If there's a corporate sigh of relief when you say, ' … and in conclusion', you've gone on too long.

Commissioner Rader also suggested that women should not be over-dramatic. Obviously, that advice did not apply to Evangeline Booth, who was known for her theatrics, but she preached in a different culture to our current one. Keep in mind the difference between breaking the bread of life and presenting a dramatic sketch or monologue. There may be room for both in our worship, but when attention is drawn to the speaker rather than to God, there's something unbalanced about our presentation.

CRITICS

When criticism comes, listen to it, reflect on it and take what God might be saying to you through it. However, don't be consumed by it. My father-in-law, now deceased, simply didn't like female preachers. He could tolerate the officer-wife's preaching, so long as it wasn't very often, but when two single women officers were sent to his corps he was furious that he would have to listen to a woman preach every week. It didn't matter whether they were expository or topical, short or long, well or ill-prepared – they were women. You might encounter a few people like that. They might have firmly-held convictions about women not speaking in church, or simply hate their mother! Remember these are their issues, not yours. You may be able to engage them in honest dialogue, or you may need – in extreme cases – to suggest kindly that they might be more comfortable worshipping in a church where women are not allowed in the pulpit. But don't let their criticism intimidate you. God has placed you in your pulpit for his purpose, not for theirs.

Don't be surprised if it is a woman who is the critic. She may have well-thought-through beliefs, or she may be jealous. Again, it is her issue, and while you can work on it with her, none of us has the power to change another person. That is between them and their Creator. In this situation it helps me to remember the profound psychological theory developed by Major Naomi Shaffer – the 'banana' theory. She tells of how monkeys are trapped in Africa. A small bamboo cage is built with a door that allows a banana to be placed inside. The bars provide enough room for the monkey to reach its hand in, but having grabbed the banana it is unable to retract its hand without letting go of the fruit. The point is: if it's your banana, hang on, but if it's not yours, let go and walk away.

THE EMPTY PULPIT

Is it ever appropriate to choose not to preach for a while? That's a hard question. There may be situations in which there are good reasons to do that. If so, it should be decided by both spouses, and would be for a limited period of time. There are times in the lives of all preachers when entering the pulpit is a serious trial, perhaps due to depression, illness, grief, or the dark night of the soul. But take care that avoiding preaching is not a means of avoiding God's touch on our life as we prepare to open his word to others.

Sometimes we are tempted to say, 'But my husband's a better preacher. Our people want to hear him.' Before you give in to that reasoning, make sure it's true. Is he better, or just different? If the roles were reversed, would he relinquish the pulpit, the platform, to you? Do you have a clear sense that this is God's will? Why? Share your thoughts with someone you trust, and see if it makes sense to them. Are you too willing to take the easy way out, or is that what should happen?

THE POWER OF THE PULPIT

As a final word of both caution and encouragement, we must always remember the power of the platform and the privilege of a Salvation Army officer as he or she stands on it. There are those in our congregations who will take every word spoken from the pulpit as the gospel truth, which places quite a burden on the speaker to be faithful to the word, and not simply to her own agenda. But, in the same sense, words spoken from the platform in the context of a caring congregation, a seeking heart and the wooing of the Holy Spirit can bring a woman, man or child to the foot of the Cross.

Six

A Square Peg in a Round Hole?

The organisation itself shouldn't become the fiddler
who plays the music to which everyone must dance.

Richard Rinehart

'I LOVE what I do day-to-day with people, but I just don't fit in the organisation.' How often I have said those words or heard them said by other women within The Salvation Army. It may be reflected in a desire to wear bright-red nail polish every day, or to reach decisions by consensus, or in ambition for leadership positions that seem less available to married women officers. It often comes when it is time to move house to accommodate a new appointment. Many women long for stability, a home to call their own, somewhere to belong where roots can be put down. Although these and other 'square peg' issues may seem small when taken alone, their cumulative effect can become overwhelming and lead to a resentment of the organisation that appears to want to squeeze them into a mould. Our goal in this chapter is to identify potential 'square peg' issues and discover ways to either sand down some of the sharp edges or develop strategies to affect personal or organisational change in the areas which cause us discomfort or limit the effectiveness of our ministry.

Deborah Flagg has described our role as fluctuating between those of Catherine Booth and Emily Dickinson. Emily found herself living 'within the narrow confines of what was acceptable for members of "the fairer sex"' while Catherine gently pushed

85

back the boundaries, in widening circles of influence, secure in her identity which came through the power of God'.

Deborah writes: 'I have experienced the confines of being a woman in a male-administered organisation, but I have also experienced wondrous possibilities for ministry. I have struggled with narrowly defined roles but have also been challenged to develop my own unique gifts ... to use Emily Dickinson's phrase, I have at times felt "softly eclipsed" by an organisation which values me, but doesn't quite know what to do with me.'

In considering ways in which women struggle to adjust to The Salvation Army's organisational structures and strictures (defined as 'an abnormal narrowing of a passage in the body' – think body of Christ), the list can be long and will vary from one woman to another. Much of what I'm writing comes from my own experience, as well as that of other women I've talked with over the years, but there are some general categories that appear to fit for us. Like other topics in this book, there will be stereotypes that may not fit all women, so take what connects with you.

A WOMAN FROM THE WORD: RAHAB
Let's look first at the example of Rahab, definitely an 'outside the box' woman of faith. Rahab was an Old Testament woman who appeared to be a square peg in a round hole. In no way did she fit the usual mould of an Old Testament heroine. We meet Rahab in the second chapter of Joshua, where she is described as a Gentile. We discover that she lived in Jericho and worked as a prostitute, probably a successful one since she had a house of her own. In the narrative we learn that she sheltered the Israelite spies, lied to the king's servants to protect them, and risked her life to help them escape. The image of the scarlet cord is forever linked with Rahab as a symbol of her courage and faith.

The story might have ended there, with the saving of her family when the walls of Jericho were demolished and the city burned, except for a few lines in the Book of Hebrews, where she became the only woman to be listed by name in the 'by faith' column of chapter 11. If all those listed in this hall of faith were gathered together in one place I can imagine Rahab, with her painted face, seductive clothing and tarnished reputation, looking around and wondering, 'Why am I here? Surely I don't belong in this company of saints.' But God took her as she was, used her mightily in the history of the people of Israel, in particular in the lineage of David and Jesus, and holds her up as a model of faith.

Why? The Scriptures tell us she was a woman of faith. She was willing to face up to the truth: 'I am living in a land whose people totally disregard the God of Israel, and I must do what needs to be done to change that.' Had it not worked, had the spies not been trustworthy, she could have been tortured and killed. She was willing to take an incredible risk based on what she believed. In the middle of that she cared for her family, exacting a promise from the spies that not only would she be protected, but her family as well. It appears that she knew who she was, and didn't waste time making apologies for that, although I'm of the view that following the destruction of Jericho, as she came to know the God she so feared, she would have come to a place of repentance and a change of lifestyle. How interesting, too, that she was willing to use her feminine wiles when appropriate to convince the king's men that the spies were gone. She did what she had to do in order to fulfill God's purpose. While she does not fit the ideal of a good Jewish woman, God used her mightily to affect change in the history of the people of Israel.

We can learn from Rahab in a variety of ways. We too need the ability to accept who we are without making excuses. We can see that it is all right to be an individual, with particular tasks to accomplish, without regard to what others say about it. While we don't want to model Rahab in her profession, we can see her as someone who did not make excuses for being a woman. It also seems that she struggled with the tension between what she was asked to do and what her family expected, but she found a way to keep them safe. Roots were important to her in her commitment to her family, and, while it may be stretching the point, salvation for her family came because they were together in Rahab's home, not scattered throughout the city. Ultimately, she found a way to work the system, negotiating for what she wanted and needed from the Israelites, as well as what was right for those she loved.

EXPRESSION OF INDIVIDUALITY

As we look at the square peg/round hole issues, perhaps one of the most apparent is the struggle to maintain a sense of individuality in an organisation which invites conformity, both in appearance and behaviour. I have a friend who, when going out to eat with a group of officers in uniform, tells the waitress, 'Our mother dressed us all alike tonight.' We all chuckle, even though we've heard it a time or two before, but underneath the chuckling, for me, there is the question, 'Who am I as an individual in the midst of this organisation?' As teenagers, often our goal as budding women is to be as like each other as possible – the same hairstyle, jeans and giggle. But maturing women begin to develop an individual personality and perhaps even a signature appearance as we become more at home in our feminine body and spirit. Since life within a quasi-military organisation can be restrictive in dress, behaviour and choice, it can be difficult to develop a distinctive identity, but it is not impossible. In the USA Eastern Territory, when I mention names such as June Rader or Cath Ditmer, those who knew these women immediately see an image of a unique woman, at ease with who she was, who found a way to be herself within the confines of the organisation.

How do we do that? It must stem initially from the transforming presence of Christ, being renewed in our mind (Romans 12:2) and flowing from an inner self of unfading beauty (1 Peter 3:4). Without these forces at work within us, any attempt at having an individual presence will be from an illegitimate place. However, when we trust Christ to renew our minds and hearts, and when we freely accept our place as daughters of the Father, we begin to blossom as women of grace.

There are many surface ways in which women within the Army have found it possible to maintain their individuality. Some decide on a hairstyle which suits them and seldom vary it, even when styles change. Others become known for their classy appearance when not in uniform. Others privately express their individuality by what they wear beneath their uniform – some even sport a hidden tattoo! It may involve choosing a particular hobby, or always having fresh flowers in their home or office – little ways to resist becoming just one anonymous person in a sea of identical uniforms. Ways of saying, 'I am me.'

AN OFFICER IN HER OWN RIGHT

On a deeper level, women who successfully address this may find a niche in a particular ministry area. While a helpmate to their husbands, they might not be willing to become simply a faceless extension of his work or identity. When I was first an officer, I was known as 'Mrs Lieutenant Lawrence Shade' and I remember wanting to scream, 'I have a Christian name too!' In those days I couldn't even write a letter to headquarters over my own signature. In that respect, at least, times have changed. I am now Major JoAnn Shade. A woman wants to be known for who she is, not as an appendage to her husband, and must find ways to graciously remind others – and herself – of that fact.

I have found it helpful to identify women within the Army whom I respect, and decide what it is that makes them unique. A favourite of mine was Brigadier Elizabeth Earl. An old-time women's social officer, Earl was, on the surface, a tough cookie, a battleaxe. She had to be, for she had a mission to care for the unwed mothers God brought her way and she often had to find ways to get around the system to achieve her mission. But what I saw, and what touched me most, was her heart that would do absolutely anything for her girls, for my children, for her Jesus – and for young lieutenants who were definitely in over their heads.

Mrs Brigadier Vangie Weyant is another woman I look to as one who found a way to sustain her identity in difficult times. I met her when she was retired and watched as she graciously cared for her beloved husband through the final stages of Parkinson's disease. She taught me a great deal about sacrificial service, given in a way that never suggested she felt she was a martyr. Hers was a grace that was contagious, as she simply did what she could for her husband and for others.

Major Sara Wittenberg also makes my list. Another retired officer in Philadelphia, she is a woman of deep conviction and courage. She had been suddenly widowed while still an active officer, and through that experience she developed a sensitive spirit of prayer and dependence upon God. Sara was a tower of strength in our corps, but in a way that was truly feminine – another woman of God who found a way to maintain her individuality while serving as an effective officer.

When you've made your own list, when you've thought about the women you know and love, ask yourself two questions. The first is: 'What draws me to them? What is it about this woman that I so much respect?' There is no need to be a copycat, but we can embrace a model of womanhood and move toward it. The second question is: 'If I was on someone else's list, what would be the key word I would want to describe me?'

One way to think about this is to look at the list of the fruit of the Spirit in Galatians 5. Instead of being overwhelmed by the task of trying to achieve all of them right now, it can be helpful to choose one fruit as your focus, so that one day Jesus can say to you, 'Well done, my cherished daughter. You have been a woman of profound gentleness (or contagious joy or unshakeable peace).' You may want to choose the one that comes most naturally, but perhaps your choice should be the one that challenges you most.

For women in their 20s and 30s, it's a time to try on different qualities, while juggling the demands of motherhood and officership. This changes as they enter their 40s, which are a time of letting go of unneeded parts of life, described by Roman Catholic nun Joyce Rupp as 'a radical, painful stripping away ... as a silent snake slipping out of an old skin that no longer fits'.

She continues: 'My "skins" have included old messages and assumptions about life that developed in my childhood, behaviours that bound me to unhealthy ways of approaching life, religious beliefs that kept my spiritual world too small, and boxed-in views of my self-identity ... Skin-shedding has brought me the task of evaluating my persona (the "faces" I show to the world) and discerning which of these, if any, need to be cast off.'

Ann Morrow Lindbergh uses a similar metaphor: 'Perhaps one can shed at this stage in life as one sheds in beach-living; one's pride, one's false ambitions, one's mask, one's armour ... Perhaps one can at last in middle age, if not earlier, be completely oneself.' Through this process, we recognise that we are not reconstructing our personality, but merely allowing God to work with us in refining our traits into women who reflect the beauty, grace and strength of God.

EMBRACING FEMININITY

Any woman who wants to function and find success within a male-dominated Movement sooner or later comes to the question: 'How can I be truly feminine within this culture?' Fifty years ago, Lindbergh wrote of the danger of buying into the male culture: 'But in our recent efforts to emancipate ourselves, to prove ourselves the equal of men, we have, naturally enough perhaps, been drawn into competing with him in his outward activities, to the neglect of our own inner springs. Why have we been seduced into abandoning the timeless inner strength of women for the temporal outer strength of men?'

Commissioner Ingrid Lindberg, a former territorial commander of Finland, has said: 'I don't think leadership, especially for women, needs to be in outward strength and presence. What is needed is inward strength: strength to dare make decisions on your own.'

I have watched over the years as women within the Army, including myself, have struggled with this. Do I have to join the 'old boys' club' to be successful within the Army? Do I need to lay aside that which makes me truly feminine in order to become someone I'm not? I spent a lot of time thinking I did, but I know now the deceptiveness of that approach. It is possible to truly embrace our femininity in healthy, holy ways and to be an effective, productive officer – although it's also true that we can choose to use our femaleness to orchestrate our own agenda in sinful ways.

Deep within me is a passion for justice, a burning desire to see women freed and systems changed; to see the playing field levelled for all people, regardless of race, gender, economic status, ancestry or ethnicity. I'm a feminist. We all have an obligation to determine where we stand in regard to the claims of feminism, recognising that there are both moderate and strident voices claiming to speak for women of faith. My convictions force me to seek both mercy and justice, to lift up the oppressed in whatever form that oppression comes and to speak for those who have no voice. Like the bent-over woman of the Gospels, or the suffragettes who chained themselves to fences to gain the vote for women, I must stand tall. If that makes me a feminist, so be it.

DEPENDENCY

This question of dependency is an important one to look at. There are practices within the Army which were put in place to facilitate the operation of the Movement's ministry but which have unintentionally created dependency, especially for women. Such things as limitations on an officer's disposable income, restrictions on earning additional income outside of officership and the lack of employment status – however justifiable some of these may be – combine to reduce the officer's personal resources, both material and psychological. It becomes easy to doubt one's ability to survive outside the Army (or without the officer-spouse), leading to a sense of 'stuckness' that is unhealthy. Rather than feeling trapped by the idea that my entire identity and my whole livelihood are wrapped up in the Army I need a healthy sense of interrelatedness and interdependence between myself and the Movement in which I serve.

THE TENSION OF ORGANISATIONAL AND FAMILY DEMANDS

In September 1982 the officers of New Jersey were gathered at Camp Tecumseh for a mandatory 'family' weekend. I obediently dropped off my baby at the designated childcare area and began crossing the bridge to the meeting area. As I walked I could hear his screams, and I found myself being torn to pieces, feeling as though I was choosing the Army over my child. It's hard to believe now that my strapping 25-year-old son was once a 'momma's boy', but he was then. As a result I spent as much time in tears that weekend as he did! It was a vivid illustration to me of the struggle mothers and wives have with the expectations of the Army.

While, in my territory at least, there is substantial flexibility within the Army for officers who are mothers, for the woman there will be times when she will feel as though she has to choose between her ministry and her family. Even though our children are now older and more self-sufficient than that crying baby, I was reminded of this tension again recently when both Larry and I were asked to serve as part of the World Trade Center disaster response and were assigned to go at the same time. It meant leaving our 11-year-old in the care of his older brothers at a time of uncertainty and anxiety for all of us.

I had to answer the questions, 'Where was I needed most?' and 'Could I trust God to provide adequately for my sons?' We went and he did, and it was an incredible experience – but not without twinges of guilt for leaving our family. It ultimately becomes a tension that must be faced with the recognition that God has given us both children and a ministry, and that he will give us what we need to care for each.

DECISION-MAKING PROCESSES

As The Salvation Army moved toward the 21st century, more opportunity for the involvement of women in the Army's leadership and decision-making process gradually came, although many feel progress has been slow. Major June Rader commented in 1980: 'For me, as a married woman, there has never been a

93

question about opportunities for ministry. But there has not been a comparable opportunity for decision-making, for functioning in a way that is coming from who I am. Now part of that says to me, I'm not really in a leadership role. I am supportive and that's good. But there are times when I think I can do something but I know that will not be my opportunity. I can only feed my ideas to somebody I think can take hold of them.'

While there has been an attempt to be more inclusive of women since June spoke those words, the structure of the Army does not lend itself well to abilities women bring to the decision-making process. As a top-down, authoritarian movement, the military model is based more on the ability to make quick decisions in the midst of battle rather than long-term planning and implementation for the growth of the organisation.

Glasser and Smalley compare sharks and dolphins in the corporate world, and the metaphor fits: '"Sharks" are stern taskmasters who relish power. Their approach is strictly top-down, leaving no doubt whatsoever about who's in charge. Theirs is a command-and-control, top-down management approach. They think with their heads, not their hearts, thereby being oblivious to employees' needs and desires. In contrast, "dolphins" are gifted motivators, excellent communicators and prefer to operate in webs rather than hierarchies. They seek respect rather than obedience from subordinates and recognise that loyalty cannot be demanded; it must be earned. They are comfortable with power, but rarely abuse it. They view themselves as leaders rather than bosses. They also prefer to build consensus whenever possible.'

Business writers Glasser and Smalley suggest that by the end of the 20th century there had been a switch in corporate America from companies run by 'sharks' to organisations that have at least some 'dolphins' in their leadership. They recognise that this paradigm switch is beneficial to women, for 'at last, women can acknowledge the fact that we are different, because different is good. Finally, we have no reason to hide our softer side for fear of being perceived as weak and powerless.'

While The Salvation Army may be still 'shark'-dominant, there is movement towards 'dolphin'-like team-building. Words like consultation, consensus, servant leadership and empowerment ran through General John Gowans's explanation on the officership changes he instituted. The difficulty for the Army is that its structure still allows for the power to be held by the occupier of one office. If the person occupying that office is an old-fashioned 'shark', that will be how he or she will operate, because the structure gives permission to do so. However, women have the ability to bring the models of consensus and team-building to the tables they are at – whether it be corps councils, finance councils or staff planning meetings. We can teach those around us that there are other ways to approach both business and spiritual decisions, and we can seek to change the approach when we hold responsibility.

ROOTS

This book was a long time in the writing; more than five years. The following paragraphs were written a while ago towards the end of a nine-year stay at a wonderful appointment, and I have decided to leave them as written, for even though my situation has changed considerably since then, they have a place in this chapter.

The older I get, the more I dread the day marching orders come. I hate the weeks that follow of packing, cleaning places in my house I didn't know existed, making address changes and preparing the farewell brief. But beyond the sheer intensity of those tasks lies the more dreaded task: pulling up roots. The thought of telling my son Daniel that it's time to leave the school he is thriving at and the friends he has made makes me both sad and mad. Saying goodbye to employees, board members and soldiers who are family to us is a duty I have no desire to undertake. While I don't necessarily feel tied to this particular set of responsibilities or to the house we live in, I am settled here, and there is a goodness about that.

I know that by nature I am not a wanderer, and I find comfort in the roots I've been able to establish in this place. The square peg in me says, 'I know what's best for my family and for myself, and

I'll tell you when it's is time to go.' The round hole counters with, 'You promised to be under orders; you're needed elsewhere and it's time to go. Trust us, and in the process trust God.'

Now I must admit I was aware of what I was getting into when I signed on (as much as a 20-year-old can comprehend these things). But for me, it is a part of the square peg/round hole dilemma where I just don't fit with what's expected within the Movement. It may not be the same for all women – some may be energised by the thought of a new home and new responsibilities – but I've talked to many women officers over the years and this seems to be one of the greatest stumbling blocks: the sense of uprootedness they feel, without much in the way of consultation, especially if the move is predicated on their husband's ability, and the wife's appointment seems to be an afterthought.

I don't believe this comes only from a selfish desire to stay put, but rather from the nesting urge God has placed within women, that calls them to protect their young and to establish a place of stability called home. Does this mean it is sometimes right to say: 'No, not now'?

Fast-forward to 2006, when my family is working to put down roots in a new community. The transition has been painful, and if I had the choice I would still be in my previous corps appointment. This is definitely the square peg/round hole scenario that wears most on me, and while systemic change around this issue is unlikely at present, perhaps it's time to do a better job supporting those who are making the moves.

METAPHOR

Another area where the square peg/round hole issue comes into play is in the use of metaphor within the Army. Metaphor is very powerful in defining an organisation, as Elizabeth A. Johnson says: 'If a religion speaks about God as a warrior, using militaristic language such as "He crushes his enemies" and summoning people to become soldiers in God's army, then the people tend to become militaristic and aggressive.'

I am not, by nature, attracted to the military metaphor. I relate to Crabb's framework (Authentic Manhood Seminar notes), as a woman who is created to wait, to invite, to receive, as opposed to the male role of moving forward, initiating, being the warrior. In that light, I am not a warrior, one who is ready to 'move across the field of battle, with conquests to be won and armed host to meet and scatter', as a song puts it. It's true that other denominations have utilised metaphors in their identity development, such as the Vineyard Church, but it may be that in using the 'army' metaphor to define The Salvation Army the metaphor has become more powerful than it should.

So, for my personal health, I must wrestle with the metaphor, as well as find ways to incorporate other metaphors into what I do and who I am. It's appropriate for a woman to realise that the warrior image may not fit her understanding of the outworking of the gospel. She can then search for metaphors which speak to her, such as the radiant, sensuous bride of Christ that he calls us to be; a midwife who comes alongside; or the living vine that speaks of growth and health.

TRIVIALISING OUR EXPERIENCE

There is a danger for women within the Army to trivialise their discomfort, setting it aside in the benefit of the larger cause of the war on sin. Writer Sue Monk Kidd speaks to her experience: 'Surely I was making a big deal out of this, I began to tell myself. So maybe there is a feminine wound in me, in women, in the Church, in the earth, but what about all those other major problems I should be concerned about – the environment, crime, war, homelessness? What is a little feminine wound by comparison? Yet the truth is, as long as one woman is dehumanised, none of us can be fully human. Trivialising our experience is a very old and shrewd way of controlling ourselves. We do it by censoring our expressions of truth or viewing them as inconsequential. We learned the technique from a culture that has practised it like an art form. The trick works like this. An image is created of a "screaming feminist" with an axe to grind. The image takes on enormous negative energy in the Church and culture. Branding a woman with this image effectively belittles her opinion and discredits it. So rather than risk the image being attached to her, a woman will often back quickly away.'

There are times when I've felt trivialised (being referred to as 'the little woman'), and there have been times when I have trivialised my own discomfort. When I consider again the square peg metaphor I realise I cannot be the only one adjusting.

WORKING WITHIN THE STRUCTURE

So what do we do when it seems as if we're selling our souls to remain a faithful soldier within the Army? Is it possible to work and minister within a movement which doesn't fit very well? Yes, because it's not the structure of the Army that touches lives, it's its spirit, its heart, its willingness to care and to serve. As long as the Army's commitment to reaching the poor, the displaced and the disenfranchised in the name of Christ remains strong I will do what I can to make the system work, and to accept its idiosyncracies, as long as they don't force me to compromise my convictions. It helps to realise no organisation will be a perfect match for everyone serving in it, and we must discover ways to find the good. It is also essential to avoid becoming a martyr or a victim, or allowing our cynicism regarding the organisational structure to seep into our ministry.

AFFECTING CHANGE

Stone Center scholar Jean Baker Miller asks: 'How do we conceive of a society organised so it permits both the development and the mutuality of all people? And how do we get there? How do women move from a powerless and devalued position to fully valued effectiveness? It would be difficult enough if we started from zero, but we do not. We start from a position in which others have power and do not hesitate to use it. Even if they do not consciously use it against women, all they have to do is remain in the position of dominance, keep doing what they are doing, and nothing will change. The women's qualities that I believe are ultimately, and at all times, valuable and essential are not the ones that make for power in the world as it is now. How then can we use these strengths to enhance our effectiveness rather than let them divert us from action?'

Miller asks a compelling question. How can we use our strength as women to become more effective, both in our ministry and in effecting change within the Movement, rather than getting tied up in our frustration? Ultimately I resort time and again to the Prayer of Serenity – asking for serenity to accept the things I cannot change, the courage to change those things I can change, and the wisdom to know the difference. Sometimes I feel as though I'm kicking a brick wall and have to accept that this is the way it is for the foreseeable future. At other times I'm able to make an impact, perhaps not as radically as I would wish, but an impact nonetheless.

WHY TRY?
There are days when I want to forget the square peg issues and just get on with it – and days when I do. Yet I realise there is more at stake in this than simply my well-being. The first is the legacy we as women are leaving to our daughters. Now I don't have any daughters myself, but I may have daughters-in-law some day, and of course there are the young women in the corps who are watching and waiting. If these women have involvement in the ministry of The Salvation Army when they are adults, what will they inherit from us?

Perhaps most important is the question of living out our faith fully. When I do not have the opportunity to fully utilise my gifts, then, like the one who buried his talent, I'm not being obedient to what God has called me to. I can whine and say, 'Oh, the Army wouldn't let me, so I couldn't.' But that's not a good enough excuse for Almighty God. I must be true to myself and my calling, and I can't let the subtle (or not so subtle) discriminatory practices of the Movement keep me from doing that.

A WOMAN OF INFLUENCE

How can women exert the influence they desire within the Army? A first step is in education, raising the consciousness of those within the Movement, whether leaders, soldiers or even our husbands. Without whining, speak of the hurts, the restrictions on leadership, the price women are paying within the Movement. We can do so through the written word, taking the time to respond to positions we disagree with, or writing articles for territorial publications. We can point out instances in which women are not being invited to the table, or in which women are assigned tasks that are stereotypical. We joke at times about men being clueless about certain things, but if they truly don't see it, it's our responsibility to help them see the various clues they are missing. And our husbands can also raise the issues when they find themselves in a position to do so.

It's perfectly appropriate to ask for what we want. If there is no female preacher in a series of meetings, we may want to suggest a woman who can do that for the next series.

In our attempt to effect change we need to be willing to pay our dues. This means responsibly assuming the tasks we're given, being prepared for meetings, and not asking for concessions because we are women. It also involves being willing to be on committees and commissions, and, at times, asking for those assignments. Often, the administrative leaders may have no idea we have an interest in particular issues, so it's helpful to them to be made aware of that interest. It may mean seeking further education, in order to contribute better to our assignments.

Whether it is in providing support for other women officers, or taking on a social issue such as pornography, welfare reform or child abuse, the Army has a rich tradition of women tackling such issues with considerable success (the 'slum sisters', for example).

Throughout the journey of officership, it's essential to be willing to fight the battles that truly matter. My rule of thumb is: 'Is this a hill I want to die on?' If it is – if it is a moral, ethical or spiritual battle which I feel strongly about – then it's worth the effort and the consequences to face it. If it's simply an issue that deals with convenience or preference, then it's one I will leave for someone else to tackle.

Deborah Flagg speaks clearly as to what is happening within the Army: 'We are currently involved in a "crisis of dismantling" in which our traditional, comfortable structures are being critically reviewed and are beginning to crumble around the edges. This dismantling is frightening for all of us, because it is the harbinger of a new world for which we may not be ready. If, however, we can begin to embrace the process, relinquish the familiar and soften the boundaries of our rigid structures, we may receive from God's hand a new way of being in which everyone – men, women, married, single officer, soldier – may begin to participate equally in the great challenge of our organisational life, our communal journey towards God.'

In the end I must stay true to who I am in Christ, as a woman called to minister within The Salvation Army. His desire is that I love him and that I love others well. If I spend my energy inappropriately fighting the structures and strictures of the Movement I will have little to give those who need the presence of Christ through my life. If I turn a blind eye to the truth of the impact of the patriarchal practices and thinking, I settle for becoming nothing more than a robot. Yet if I can find ways that graciously speak to the needs of my heart, as well as to the needs of other women, I will have made an impact of lasting value.

Seven

PKs and Prodigals

Little Billy's mother was always telling him
exactly what he was allowed to do
and what he was not allowed to do.
All the things he was allowed to do were boring.
All the things he was not allowed to do were exciting.
One of the things he was NEVER NEVER allowed to do,
the most exciting of them all,
was to go out through the garden gate
all by himself and explore the world beyond.

Roald Dahl, *The Minpins*

AS a family living in the fishbowl of officership, we've had our fair share of embarrassing moments. Our oldest son, Greg, was not too excited about attending the Sunday evening service: 'Church again?' We lived directly behind the corps building, so I let him play in the yard while I went to the meeting (mistake number one), his father being out of town at a conference. Greg, in his infinite seven-year-old boy wisdom, climbed the backyard tree with a rope in his mouth (mistake number two), lost his balance and fell, causing the rope to dislodge his front tooth, so that it protruded at a right angle from his mouth. He ran into the hall as I was preaching, with blood flowing freely from his mouth, wailing like a banshee. At that moment I would have preferred to be anywhere else but there!

Those moments of public stress have been balanced out during our years as parents by many wonderful times, such as when, like

103

all the other parents, we've enjoyed my favourite autumn pastime, cheering in the stands as our sons have played football at school. We shed our officers' uniforms and headed to the football field, ready to yell our lungs out. I cherish those times of simply being 'mom' without having to worry who was watching us or needed our attention.

Most of the time, though, our parenting lives as officers are played out in the fishbowl, the public eye. We face the typical PK (preachers' kids) issues, as well as some that are unique to officership. We wrestle with the tension between being a parent and being an officer, and the choices that have to be made in that tension. Perhaps this is the most difficult chapter for me to write, as there are deep sorrows for me as to the parenting choices I made. Too often I chose the Army (and my own ambition and drivenness) over my children. While finding the balance between being a committed officer and an effective parent is not an easy task, we have a responsibility to both covenants, and proactively considering the foundations for our decisions can help to minimise our regrets at the finish.

I'm not outlining a plan for parenting in this chapter, as there are many helpful resources on that subject, but I want to raise the issues that officer mothers – and fathers – face as they navigate their children's teenage and young adult years. Framing our discussion in this chapter are the words of Christian psychologist Larry Crabb: 'After you've read the best book available on any topic involving relationship, you still face situations that require a courage and trust that can come only from a personal walk with God . . . The key to becoming a more effective parent is to become a more godly person.'

A FAMILY FROM THE WORD

An ancient biblical family faced similar issues to officer families. In today's terminology, David's family was a blended family, but they didn't blend very well. I won't attempt a family tree, suffice it to say that David had at least 20 children who are named in the

Scriptures, from at least seven different mothers, and (bearing in mind the 50-50 odds on having boys or girls) there must surely have been more daughters than the only one named, Tamar. David's deepest heartache surrounded the children of Maacah (Tamar and Absalom), Bathsheeba (unnamed infant who died at birth, Solomon, Jedidiah and Shammua), and Ahinoam (Amnon). While the cultural setting is different from ours, we can certainly learn from their pain.

REGARD FOR CHILDREN

What was the status of children within this family? Clearly, favouritism was at work. David favoured Amnon as his firstborn, and Solomon had an advantaged position as David's chosen successor – in fact, while David named him Solomon, God named him Jedidiah, meaning 'the Lord's beloved'. It's also possible that certain children were favoured because of who their mothers were. Tellingly, the most caring interaction recorded in the Scriptures between David and a child was not with his own son but with Jonathan's son, Mephibosheth. Did his own children question whether he cared more about Jonathan's son than his own?

Four incidents speak of David's struggles with Absalom, beginning with Absalom's outrage at the rape of his sister and David's subsequent unwillingness to intervene. When Absalom killed Amnon to avenge his sister's rape, Absalom went into exile for three years. David longed for Absalom during that time, but did not allow him to return until after Joab's intervention. Even then David would not see Absalom, and two years later Absalom was out 'burning the fields' to get his father's attention. In their last interaction, occurring through their respective armies, David and Absalom were at odds with each other as they battled militarily. David's confusion regarding his son was obvious when David urged his commanders Joab, Abishai and Ittai: 'Be gentle with the young man Absalom for my sake', even though they were at war against each other (2 Samuel 18:5 *TNIV*).

When news of Absalom's death reached David, he mourned deeply: 'O my son Absalom! My son, my son Absalom! If only I had died instead of you – O Absalom, my son, my son' (2 Samuel 18:33 *TNIV*). Joab chastises David for choosing his son over the nation, and spoke again of David's seeming ambivalence (2 Samuel 19:6 *TNIV*): 'You love those who hate you and hate those who love you' – a tragic comment about the king. David may have loved his children but he did not set limits for them, and he and they paid a high price for that failure.

FACING THE TRUTH

David's unwillingness to face the truth cost his family dearly, especially when David's son Amnon fell in love with his half-sister Tamar, 'the beautiful sister of David's son Absalom' (2 Samuel 13:1). Where was Maacah, Tamar's mother? Where was Ahinoam, Amnon's mother? Where was David? Was no one paying attention to what was happening? It's hard to believe that David was clueless about what was going on – Amnon didn't appear to be hiding his feelings from those around him. Yet David sent Tamar to Amnon's bedroom! (2 Samuel 13:7). Tamar was raped by Amnon, and David apparently did nothing. Oh, 'When King David heard all this, he was furious' (verse 21) but he didn't punish Amnon because he favoured him as his firstborn son. And David's unwillingness to deal with the problem ultimately resulted in Amnon's death at the hands of his brother Absalom, and the devastation of Tamar.

GODLY PARENT

What can we learn from this tragic family history? It's apparent that being 'a man (or woman) after God's own heart' does not necessarily lead to good parenting skills, nor does it exempt us from parenting difficulties. Officers sometimes say: 'I believe God has called me to be an officer, and I will trust him to take care of my children.' While there's nothing inherently untrue in that statement, it cannot serve as an abdication of our responsibility

106

to parent our children well. Yes, God loves our children even more than we do, but he has entrusted them to us, both to nurture and to discipline, and we cannot deny that sacred responsibility.

SIN AND GUILT

David's story also shows us that sin and guilt have long-lasting results. Did David's parenting failures stem in part from his sin with Bathsheeba and his guilt over the death of their first child? Was Amnon allowed to do as he pleased because he was the firstborn surviving child or because David's beloved firstborn had died? Was David's disregard of Bathsheeba – and perhaps women in general – the root of his disregard for Tamar? While each individual has responsibility for his or her own actions, patterns develop within family life which lead to generational sin. Our responsibility to our children is to break those patterns as well as to be aware of how unrepentant sin and consuming guilt can detrimentally affect those we love.

BURNING THE FIELDS

We also learn from David that children raised without time, energy, commitment and love may very well resort to 'burning the fields' to get our attention. While the actual number of hours spent with our children and the quality of our parenting matter, if our children perceive that the Army gets the lion's share of us – or has a deeper claim on our hearts – they will be out 'burning the fields' or turning to other avenues to get the attention they crave. 'Acting out' sends a message: 'I'm angry, I'm scared, I'm lonely, I'm hurt.' As parents we need to recognise the acting out and respond with restorative dialogue.

FAVOURITES

There's a danger in giving uneven status and regard to our children as David did. Perhaps one child fits into Salvation Army culture better – musically talented, leadership skills. Or perhaps one is an 'easier' child, or more like you or their father. Families must work hard at being inclusive of all their members, regardless of interests or personalities.

A BLIND EYE

A critical lesson from David is that we cannot turn a blind eye to the family dynamics unfolding around us. I'm outraged that a father would allow his daughter to be raped by his son and do nothing about it. Each one of the children in the family has a right to be protected. While confronting situations which need intervention is often difficult, problems and conflicts won't go away on their own. They will get worse if ignored. We can't put our children at risk because we are unaware of what is going on or choose to ignore it. We sin against them when we turn a blind eye to what is true.

THE HARD STUFF

Officers' children face some unique challenges. Someone once made a list: You Know You're an Officers' Kid When . . .

1   You play a brass instrument nobody has heard of.
2   You take your driving test in a minibus.
3   Everyone you know has initials: DC, YPSM, CO, CSM.
4   All your romances take place at camp.
5   You're frequently a sermon illustration.
6   Your friends say, 'Yeah, but where do you go to church?'
7   During December, the drive-through staff at McDonald's call your parents by name.
8   After living in a house for three years you get the uncontrollable urge to pack.

While we laugh at this, the list suggests some deeper concerns. Studying Canadian clergy families, Douglas Campbell asked adult children of pastors to speak about the negative aspects of growing up in the parsonage, and they pointed to a number of problems: their parents being on call, being exposed to too much religion, experiencing an initial negative response from other children in school and the neighbourhood, unrealistic community expectations. In addition, our children have to face other issues, such as the enmeshment of roles, being 'on stage', financial pressures, frequent moves and derision from their peers. Here in the USA, it would not be unusual for them to hear, on the bus travelling to a high school football game, the refrain: 'Salvation Army, Salvation Army, put a nickel in the drum, save another drunken bum.' In the United Kingdom, I understand, there's a similar chant: 'Salvation Army, all gone barmy, going up to Heaven in a biscuit tin.'

ENMESHMENT

The issues of enmeshment spill over from officer marriages to officer families. Where is the dividing line between who we are as an officer and who we are as a parent? As a pre-schooler, Greg tried in vain to get his father's attention: 'Dad … DAD!', finally yelling, 'Lieutenant!' Only then did he get his father's attention!

While family involvement in the corps is healthy, officer parents must decide how much to involve their children in their ministry. Some officers regard Army ministry as a 'family affair' but, especially as they get older, our children need room for their own choices. How much 'work' – in briefcases, on computer screens and in meal-time discussions – do we bring home, and how much can we leave at the corps? The walls do have ears, and even small children can piece together too much of what is happening in the corps than is good for them to know. And sometimes blurt it out at the worst time! There must be times when the officer persona gets shelved and we are simply 'mom'.

THE MODEL CHILD

The officers' child runs the risk of being held up to the corps congregation as a model child. This pressure may come from the congregation itself, but often it reflects on the expectations of the officer parents. What does it feel like for your child to wear his junior soldier uniform when the rest of the children are wearing football shirts to the meeting? Are you holding your teenagers up as paragons of virtue, forcing them to sneak around rather than be open with you about their struggles?

Living as the corps officers' child does put the whole family's life on display. What do you do when they misbehave in the holiness meeting? How do you respond to their mouthy response when others are watching? While it's unlikely that our children can remain incognito during our stay in a corps appointment, I appreciate the message of *Leadership* contributor Pastor Michael Phillips: 'Recently a new church member observed, "I don't even know which children are your kids." I snared one of my children from the throng of hooligans and introduced my ruffian. I smiled inwardly at our secret identity. My children do not have to be better – or better known – than any one else's. More than anything, I want my children to be blessed through my ministry, not condemned. Our sensitivity to the unique expectations placed on our children will go a long way toward keeping bitterness from seeping into the family.'

Our unwillingness to hold our children up as role models, as well as our desire that they be treated as normal corps kids, will go a long way to normalising their faith experiences.

FINANCIAL ISSUES

Officer parents and their children often live in a middle-class setting but have limited financial resources. That makes paying for expensive school trips a real sacrifice for the family budget, and one they may choose not to make. When my son Dan tells me about all the 'stuff' his friends have, it gives me the opportunity to talk about values, money and how we express our care for each other. We learn together that wants are not the same as needs. Even if I had more expendable cash, I wouldn't have purchased those items for my son, but the financial pressure of having limitations on any additional earnings can make the contrast of lifestyles difficult.

TIME

Tensions over time will always exist. Officers' flexibility over the management of their time is offset by demands on their time which can frustrate family members. Our children wonder why Mom has to stay late at the office, be with someone who needs her, or go off to the annual retreat without them. A variable schedule presents additional complications. If we could tell them we will be home at exactly 5.30 pm, they could count on us being there. But unexpected circumstances make our schedule unpredictable, and that's hard on our children. We can address this somewhat by better defining 'emergencies' and setting more restrictive boundaries around our availability if necessary.

MOVING

Of all the issues of officership which have an impact on our children, it's the frequent house moves which appear to take the largest toll on them. I recently heard an officer talk about his childhood as the child of officers, telling how he attended nine different schools as they moved from place to place. This lack of stability places an even larger burden upon the parents to make the family a stabilising unit. If the time the family spends together at home is unpredictable, and the location changes every two or three years, where do our children find their equilibrium?

The frequent moves can affect the children academically, and can cause them to have difficulty establishing and maintaining relationships. Our young-adult sons have strongly articulated their hope that their younger brother would not experience as much change as they did. During a time of uncertainty regarding our Salvation Army appointment our oldest son Greg said, 'When I changed schools twice within two years when I was starting high school I never really fitted in again. I don't want Daniel to have to go through that.' I heard that message, painful as it was, and have had to find a way to balance what's best for my children with what's needed for the ministry I've made a commitment to.

CROSS-CULTURAL SETTINGS

Some officer appointments require the family to function in cross-cultural settings. The challenges presented by a 'missions' assignment in a developing territory are obvious, but there are also homeland appointments, even within the division in which we serve, which ask our children to be part of a worship experience and social interactions that are foreign to them. It may be a change from suburban to rural to urban, to a different socio-economic status group, or to a different racial grouping than our own. We spent a number of years in corps that were racially integrated only by the presence of our family and one or two others, and those years brought unique blessings and challenges to our parenting.

Our youngest son, Daniel, was the only Caucasian child in his day care centre, a part of our ministry in Cleveland Hough, and I was reminded of its impact on him when we stood at the fast food counter in the mall one day. He was about two, and he stood singing at the top of his little lungs, 'We shall overcome, we shall overcome some day . . .' It was Black History Month and the day care children were learning the songs of their history – as was my little blond boy. While he probably had no understanding of what he was singing, it helped me connect with the heritage of the people God had entrusted to our care for him to be able to sing along in their continued seeking of economic and social freedom.

As our boys moved toward their teenage years we had to decide how much freedom to give them in that inner city neighbourhood. Some of the youngsters coming to the centre were already involved in gangs and drug sales – could we trust our boys not to have interactions with them? Who would influence whom? There were questions of safety in the neighbourhood, and I would hold my breath when Greg walked to 'Grandpa's', the neighborhood greasy spoon cafe, for chicken wings, knowing that, even though he was with a friend, there had been a murder at the store down the block just that week. We wanted to continue our practice of involving our boys in the life of the corps, but the cross-cultural setting raised new questions for us.

112

HOW INVOLVED?

What about when they don't want to go to the meetings with you? Do you make them go? Anne Lamott writes about her desire to have her son attend church with her: 'You might wonder why I make this strapping, exuberant boy come with me most weeks, and if you were to ask, this is what I would say. I make him because I can. I outweigh him by nearly 75 pounds. But that is only part of it. The main reason is that I want to give him what I found in the world, which is a path and a light to see by. Most of the people I know who have what I want – which is to say, purpose, heart, balance, gratitude, joy – are people with a deep sense of spirituality. They are people in community, who pray, or practise their faith . . . They follow a brighter light than the glimmer of their own candle; they are part of something beautiful.'

I want that for my children; I want them to be a part of the corps community, and I want them to know Jesus.

WHEN THEY DON'T FIT IN

As they grow into adolescence, when we no longer outweigh them, the question gets harder. What if they don't fit in at the corps? Might there come a time when they need to be encouraged to find another faith fellowship? Maybe they've had enough, and want time to step away from the Army. What do we demand of them, what do we invite them to? When our older sons were in their late teens we were blessed by a soldier in our corps who truly understood this and who was a supporting voice when others expressed opinions about the whereabouts of the officers' children. When we were the prayer family of the week, he prayed sensitively for our sons, acknowledging our ache at their absence. While we would like our children to share in our faith tradition, I'm reminded of the wall hanging that has been in our home since the boys were small: 'There are two lasting gifts we give our children: the first, roots; the second, wings.' I've come to realise that God calls me to trust him more and more for my children as they grow and expand their wings, as I step aside and watch them choose their paths. As

Evangeline Paterson prays in 'A Wish for my Children': 'May you grow strong to break all the webs of my weaving.'

WHERE IS HOME?
In mid-June, our son Dan went to work at camp for the summer, and came home in August to a new house, furniture, neighbourhood and school. Other officers' kids have enrolled in community college only to have their parents appointed three states away halfway through their first year. Home no longer looks the same. One way many youngsters have found to establish a sense of ownership through the years has been to carve or paint their initials somewhere in their home. But it still doesn't help the problem of a young adult not having a place to call home, a place which brings back memories.

ENLARGING EXPERIENCES
Let's be positive! Life as an officers' child has great value as well. Our children have benefited richly through the years through being exposed to experiences unique to the ministry.

They learn how to interact with people from various economic levels, from the poor in the soup kitchen to the wealthy members of our advisory boards. Philadelphia Roxborough Corps was multicultural, and the boys learned to play 'stone, paper, scissors' in Chinese with a student from Hong Kong, visited Canadian soldiers in their Toronto home, chatted with a young doctor from Zimbabwe as he shared dinner in our home, and got to know the divisional leaders, Lieut-Colonels Paul and Kay Rader, who later became international leaders of The Salvation Army.

They also learned what it was like to be marginalised. Many of the children who attended corps activities were poor, some had alcoholic parents and others suffered from the prejudiced behaviour of others. They went with their black friends into the convenience store and watched the clerk scrutinise them the whole time they were there. They asked their unanswerable questions when one of the children in the centre was beaten to death by his mother. They saw at first hand the effects of drug addiction, as a man in rehab who attended our meetings and played the drum relapsed time and again.

BROAD HORIZONS
Their experiences have definitely had an impact on their cultural awareness. Greg was involved in racial awareness training at his school, and the instructor asked all the African-American kids to go to one side of the room and all the white kids to go to the other. Greg said to me, 'Mom, I just sat in my seat, 'cause I belonged on both sides.' He felt a very close connection with the African-American people we ministered to, and even to this day can very easily slip into the ghetto idiom he learned during his years in Hough, and is sensitive to prejudicial feelings and behaviours.

A UNIQUE FELLOWSHIP
Our children also have the privilege of being part of the unique Army fellowship, even if they do not choose to continue to worship in Army corps. We've known a number of young-adult children of officers over the years who have chosen other avenues of worship and service, but later sought out the local corps for ways to keep in touch with their roots. One visits a local nursing home each Christmas with her family as a part of the League of Mercy, another made it a point to play his brass instrument during Christmas street collections, challenging his siblings to match his hourly rate in the communities they lived in. Others have served on advisory boards or helped with children's activities.

WHAT MATTERS
In looking at all of these difficulties and benefits I can't help but wonder what makes the difference. Are there things we can do as parents that will continue to nurture our children in the faith and help prevent them becoming bitter toward the Army? David Goetz researched the subject and found some common characteristics among pastors whose families have thrived in ministry. They are a

115

family protector, making 'a concerted effort to protect their spouse and children from the various pressures that accompany ministry'. They are psychologically aware, understanding their own tendency toward 'drivenness, workaholism or an obsession with high approval ratings', and their propensity to have a rescue mentality. Speaking to the enmeshment issue he uses the example of a pastor father who 'couldn't draw the line between being a father and being his son's saviour'. His final indicator is that they are able to be a family cheerleader, encouraging 'their family members' involvements beyond the church'.

Michael Phillips adds the caution that 'bitterness is a communicable disease', saying: 'I must learn to season my ministry with grace, and in doing so pass on a grace legacy to my children.' As parents live a consistent life based on Kingdom values, these values will be transferable to their children. No guarantees, but there are none in life anyway, simply the promise that the God who gave us our children will continue to love them.

GETTING PRACTICAL

What to do? Parenting teenagers is not easy, no matter what, and techniques only go so far. Crabb sums up what is needed: 'Involvement when it's pushed away, a tender spirit in response to meanness, a warm resolve to do good to someone who's breaking your heart, discipline administered firmly (not hatefully) even at times when it will likely provoke vicious defiance in your teenager, quiet hope that continues to believe in someone after repeated failure – all this and more, much more, is involved in grace. Being a gracious person matters more than understanding internal dynamics or having regular devotions or spending quality time with your kids. Those things matter, but without a love fueled by grace they add up to nothing.'

WHEN IT GOES WRONG

In *The Officer* magazine, Barbara Robinson wrote: 'There is little more agonising to officer parents than the child who turns away

116

from God – who chooses a lifestyle radically removed from Kingdom values.'

'Train up a child in the way he should go' is proverbial wisdom, but not a set-in-stone guarantee. When an adolescent or young adult chooses to move in a radically different direction, struggles with mental illness or gets tied up in addictions, we, as onlookers, find ourselves asking a question similar to the disciples in John 9:2 (*TNIV*): 'Rabbi, who sinned, this man or his parents, that he was born blind?' We wonder what went wrong, how the parents failed to raise the child well, who is at fault. And as the parents of such a child, we ask the same questions.

The blame and shame games can overwhelm, but we can choose to maturely own the responsibility for our behaviour, recognising that we cannot control the outcome of another's life. We pray passionately that God will place a hedge around our children and protect them from danger. And we must remember that love continues to believe the best about another, unless there is solid evidence to the contrary.

PARENTS IN PAIN

In *Parents in Pain*, psychologist John White outlines the necessity of living in a spirit of relinquishment when our children are walking in paths that are far from home and far from God. This spirit includes releasing the right to be proud, being willing to forego any repayment for what you have done for your children, giving up your right to respectability, allowing your children to face pain and trusting God about your children rather than trusting your own ability to manage their lives.

His are sobering words, but full of wisdom, especially as we make the distinction between how much of our pain is about the child and how much it is about us. We might want to crawl into bed and pull the covers over our head because of our shame over their actions, but we are challenged to remember that the father in Jesus' story of the prodigal did not cower in shame but watched and waited for his son to return home, running to him as he walked up the road.

DISCLOSURE

When our children get into trouble we may shy away from letting others know of their situation. But the Army grapevine makes that difficult, even when the story is shared in hopes of prayer support. There doesn't seem to be one good way of handling gossip, but a simple statement which gives the minimum of information but an indication of the depth of the pain involved for the entire family may be appropriate. Others who have had, or are having, similar experiences can be sought out for mutual support. This is the time to draw upon those people in your life whom you can call and say, 'Please pray for our family. I don't want to go into details but I need to know you are praying.'

THE PRODIGAL

What of the ongoing relationship with the prodigal and the rest of the family? Honest interaction continues to be essential. Forbidden behaviour can be tempting for our children, and an older sibling may be a heroic figure our other children want to emulate. Or the disruption of the prodigal, whether in or out of the home, may be causing uproar. Our response cannot be naive, but it must find ways to be supportive. When it's our own child we lose perspective, so this is often a time to look for help from professional sources, because we are not invincible and need to be able to receive as well as to give. While we never want to turn off the porch light, there may, in the most extreme cases, come a time when we must say: 'You cannot live with us anymore. Your influence on the rest of this family is too dangerous for you to continue to wield it.'

In the midst of that pain it's vital to remember that as much as we love that child, as much as we would make many sacrifices for him or her, God loves them so much more, and made the ultimate sacrifice for them through the death of Christ. As part of the dedication ceremony for our child we entrusted him or her to God, and we cannot take that back into our own hands. It can be one of the biggest tests of our faith, one that may last for years, but knowing God continues to call them home can bring some comfort to us.

BLAMING THE ARMY

How easy it can be to blame the Army for our children's circumstances! I found myself doing this recently when I was privileged to be a part of the ministry of Pendel Brass and Singers, musical groups from the division we had been stationed in when the boys were young. I began to play the 'if only' game. If only we hadn't been moved to Ohio from Philadelphia our boys would have had the experience of being in Pendel, and might be upstanding young adult members of that band and of the Army, instead of their current fringe involvement. If only the Army didn't expect so much of me. If only the Army cared more about our children. If only . . . Again, the shame and blame games can be deadly, for they don't lead anywhere. We need to face what is true and move forward from there with the grace of God enabling us to accept what is.

John Townsend puts it like this: 'We ... need to make certain we don't adopt the victim mentality ... A victim says, "Hey, this wasn't my fault. Now somebody take care of me." A healthy person will say instead, "This may not have been my fault, but it's my responsibility to get better." Those people who take responsibility for their lives end up doing much better than those who are filled with envy, blame and a sense of loss of control over their lives.'

KEEPING THE LIGHT ON

While I've been speaking in generalities, the question arises in specific situations: 'How much is enough?' Wayne Watson sings a poignant song that touches that question: 'And you pray to keep from worrying and you worry you ain't praying enough.' Perhaps the most telling of the research Douglas F. Campbell has done on adult PKs is found in answer to his question: 'What would you have changed about your experience as a pastor's kid?' Their first answer: they wanted a closer relationship with the clergy parent.

Just as the quality of the therapeutic relationship between counsellor and client is of more value than specific psychological techniques, so too the parental relationship with the child will remain foremost in their mind and influence, regardless of the number of appointments, the type of discipline used, or the rank attained. Keep the light on!

Eight

Can I Find – and Keep – a Centre?

*In the midst of noise and confusion we are settled into
a deep inner silence.*

Richard Foster

A WOMAN Salvation Army officer's life can be like the circus performer keeping a dozen plates spinning at the top of poles balanced on various parts of his body. The metaphor is most fitting during the child-rearing years, coordinating school schedules, homework, corps programming, community involvement, baby-sitting, car pools and the needs of our husbands with our personal and spiritual needs. Even for women who have no children, or those whose children no longer live at home, the number of plates we spin can feel overwhelming. William James describes it as the German *zerrissenhart*, which means 'torn-to-pieces-hood' – the feeling that everybody wants a piece of us, until there is nothing left to be divided up.

Various strategies can reduce the number of plates or the speed required to keep them spinning, such as time management techniques or delegating responsibilities to others, but they are not enough in themselves to keep our souls intact. We fear becoming the woman who Christian writer Ruth Senter describes: 'She is today's modern woman. God has blessed her with systems for doing love ... Punctual. Precise. Efficient, but void of spirit, lacking heart, out of tune ... The One who knows her best knows that she is a song without melody, a well without water. There is no spirit to her day, only schedule. No heart, only habit. No sense of wonder or quiet contemplation, only compulsion to work … No messages of love direct from the One who loves her most, only noise and clamour and someone else's thoughts about love.'

To rediscover that sense of wonder, the quiet contemplation our souls innately long for, we need a centred life, with an internal locus of control so we do not become lost in chaos. It is a centre which flows from the Spirit of God dwelling within us, and which is cared for as the proverb urges: 'Above all else, guard your heart, for it is the wellspring of life' (Proverbs 4:23 *NIV*).

WOMEN FROM THE WORD: MARY AND MARTHA

Martha and Mary, who appear in the Gospel of Luke, are sisters with two different priorities in life. Note what happened: 'As Jesus and his disciples were on their way, he came to a village where a woman named Martha opened her home to him. She had a sister called Mary, who sat at the Lord's feet listening to what he said. But Martha was distracted by all the preparations that had to be made. She came to him and asked, "Lord, don't you care that my sister has left me to do the work by myself? Tell her to help me!"

'"Martha, Martha," the Lord answered, "you are worried and upset about many things, but only one thing is needed. Mary has chosen what is better, and it will not be taken away from her"' (Luke 10:38-42 *TNIV*).

We can visualise the scene: Martha in the heat of the kitchen, running back and forth to meet the needs of this hungry group of visitors. Resentment begins to build in Martha, as Mary sits, absorbed in Jesus' words, ignoring her sister's pointed glare. Imagine the strident tone of Martha's voice, demanding that Jesus correct this perceived injustice. 'It's not fair,' she insists, 'I need help.'

But Jesus did not match her tone in his response; in fact, I can picture him gently touching Martha's hands, looking at her deeply and speaking truth to her heart. He exposed her absorption with the distractions and led her back to what her heart was longing for – his presence.

In contrast, Mary is at the feet of Christ, choosing 'the better part'. She is found there in two other instances of Scripture, falling at Jesus' feet in her grief over the death of her brother Lazarus (John 11) and anointing his feet in preparation for his death (John 12). In each setting, her response is welcomed by Jesus. Mary may have been contemplative by nature, able to sit and drink in, hungry to worship. However, based on Jesus' comment in this passage, it's just as likely that her actions were a direct result of her choice, of her awareness that being at the feet of Christ when he was near her was all she could do.

While I can't knock Mary's devotion to the Lord I resent the fact that Martha has taken all the criticism over 2,000 years of commentaries and preaching, because there is much of Martha in me – and in most Salvation Army women. We have a mission, a calling to fulfill, and that takes work to accomplish. There are people to feed, feet to wash, and lives to touch – and that includes time in the kitchen. We've heard this story for years, you and I, and in the hearing it is essential to recognise that it was not Martha's work in itself that Christ was concerned with – it was her all-consuming preoccupation with it.

Christ speaks to the difference between distractions and focus, between doing and being. His words do not give us a pass on fulfilling the commitment to ministry that we have made, but are a vivid reminder that without the sitting, without the centre, we are only a bundle of distractions, running here and there with little of substance to give anyone else.

Devotional writer Ken Gire describes it this way: 'We find ourselves in an inner tug of war, pulled one way by our duties and another way be our devotion. There was no quiet centre that Martha was working from – no solitude of heart, no still axis around which her activities revolved.'

A TWENTY-FIRST CENTURY MARY

The image of a centred woman in today's world is one who knows how to feed her soul. Her calendar may be of a modern-day Martha or Mary but the external activity does not define a woman who has a deep spiritual centre. She may be a high-profile leader or a quiet spirit who moves behind the scenes but it is her capacity not to be shaken in the core of who she is that enables her to provide a sense of stability to those around her. There is a sense of presence about her, the dignity of the inner self that Peter alludes to in 1 Peter 3, the unfading beauty of a gentle and quiet spirit, 'unanxious and unintimidated' (*The Message*).

TO A CENTRE

How do we get there, with all the demands placed upon us in the Army and which we place upon ourselves? Tell me the steps, and I'll be sure to accomplish this. I'll make it my goal for the month. Warning, warning – steps won't get you there. Presence is the only route to spiritual centredness. It begins with desire, recognising that our hearts long for a centredness, a sense of self and of Spirit that is one. In our culture we can deceive ourselves that all is well, for skill at plate-spinning keeps us looking good to others and too busy and bombarded to hear any other voice.

In our relationship with God, some of us have been able to find and maintain what is needed. But others need Elijah's broom tree experience of desperation (1 Kings 19) to awaken the need to go to the mountain, to the presence of the Lord. The desire for the One we love is within us – we choose to meet him. My spiritual director reminded me recently that on every journey there is a time to stop and dig a well. So climb the mountain or grab the shovel, and be ready for God.

GETTING READY

Barbara Metz and John Burchill give us good guidance: 'When we think of centring, it is important to acknowledge the state we often find ourselves in as we come to prayer. It is the state in which we experience life. We do not hear the music of life. It is a background of which we are unaware. We do not see the stars because there is so much brightness and attraction in the complexity of our daily living. We do not smell the flowers. There simply isn't time. We do not touch our own centre. We are, by the pace of life, hurried on to the next experience before we can go deeply into our feeling and being.'

The goal of centring is to 'seek an ability to attend to what is deeper, an ability to dwell upon the reality of God. We seek an ability to exclude what is irrelevant and superficial and open ourselves to the relevant truth of things and attend to a development of a presence.'

TIME

In our instant society we want immediate results, but centredness demands time – both quantity and quality. It's time that must be carved out rather than snatched, for it demands something of us. I find that ultimately I make time for what is important, for what brings me pleasure, for what is rewarding in some way. And this is probably true for you as well. Anything worth having in life comes with a cost, and this sense of centredness is no exception. It can be small units of time, or great blocks, but it must get priority. If our response is: 'There's no way I can squeeze one more thing into my day', then we're not ready. Pray that God will continue to woo you with his unrelenting Spirit towards this end.

Do not be discouraged when the going seems slow or the time seems barren. If you are anticipating the day when you wake up with the exclamation: 'I'm centred. Wow! Now I don't have to make this a priority anymore. I've made it' – not! The Christian life doesn't work that way. For as you experience the Spirit's invitation and begin to respond you will be more aware of how deep the hunger is.

SOLITUDE

We do not need to be afraid of being alone (loneliness) or being absorbed in the clatter of our world, says Quaker writer Richard Foster. We can 'cultivate an inner solitude and silence that sets us free from loneliness and fear'. Psychologist Brenda Hunter describes it as having 'enough fallow time to have peace of mind and enjoy sweet sleep ... where life is lived calmly, richly, deeply – a refuge in a frantic world'.

Henri Nouwen writes of solitude: 'Solitude is the place of conversion, the place where the old self dies and the new self is born. In solitude I get rid of my scaffolding (the desire to run to my distractions). The struggle is far, far beyond our own strength ... We have to fashion our own desert where we can withdraw every day, shake off our compulsions and dwell in the gentle healing presence of our Lord. Without such a desert we will lose our own soul while preaching the gospel to others. Our task is to help people concentrate on the real but often hidden event of God's active presence in their lives – the creation of a space where communion becomes possible and community can develop.'

I can hear your reaction already: 'There's no way I can find a place of solitude in my busy life. You just don't know what's going on for me.' I know, I've been there, and still am there more than I wish. But what I also know is that when I can't find that space, that quiet, I pay a heavy price.

Anne Morrow Lindberg, writing in 1955, understood how the need for solitude affects women: 'It is more a question of inner convictions than of outer pressure [that keeps us from seeking solitude]. Certain springs are tapped only when we are alone ... women need solitude in order to find again the true essence of themselves: that firm strand which will be the indispensable centre of a whole web of human relationship. The problem is not entirely in finding the room of one's own, the time alone, difficult and necessary as this is. The problem is more how to still the soul in the midst of its activities. In fact the problem is how to feed the soul.'

We don't need to start with a week of silence in a monastery or retreat setting to experience solitude. It's found in those first minutes of the dawning, when the sun creeps through the window and wakes us before the alarm shrills its noisy wake-up call; or in the quiet of the car, driving to work when we deliberately turn off the radio and settle into the stillness; or in the small hours of the

126

night when the baby has been soothed and you sit with him in your arms, rocking to the rhythm of his gentle breathing; or you slip out to the porch or into the garden as the stars shine in their glorious canopy. At such times little solitudes await us. Solitude cultivates the ability to live in the moment, seeing with eyes that search for the 'little solitudes', with noses sensitive to the obvious roses and less-obtrusive lilies of the valley, and ears eager for the whisper on the wind.

Solitude is enhanced by welcoming space. A favourite cartoon of mine depicts a living room with children running around, and the mother sitting under an overturned playpen.

Our sacred space may be a room, a chair, a do-not-disturb sign on your office door and phone, or even a few minutes in the bath tub with the door locked. A quiet place can block out the world for a few moments and allow the consuming clamour to be hushed.

As the desire for solitude increases it may be possible to schedule some time away. A friend of mine recently did this. She asked her husband to care for the children for 24 hours and went to a local retreat centre, where for a small charge she was able to spend those 24 hours alone: reading, praying, fasting, listening and, yes, sleeping without having an ear open for her children's cries. As she related her experience, a deepened centredness reflecting the presence of God was apparent.

Such times away can be life-changing. When I attended a conference in San Diego I deliberately skipped the site visits and the evening dinner to catch a bus to the ocean, to La Jolla. I walked along the beach, with the messages of the waves washing over my weary soul. I finally sat quietly, peacefully, with the sun setting on the horizon in front of me, sharing in the solitary breaking of bread in the presence of Christ. Did I plan it that way when I went to San Diego? No, but the Spirit knew the way.

Another opportunity came while driving along Route 80, passing through the Delaware Water Gap as music poured from the cassette player. I was experiencing a crisis in faith and had spent considerable time on that trip praying and seeking the Lord in repentance and sorrow. As the vista opened before me I saw an incredibly awesome landscape of power and majesty, with the blazing sun streaming down upon it. 'This is My Father's World' was the song (*SASB* 42) coming from the car speakers: 'O let me ne'er forget ... I saw him once again for who he was – and is.'

'Beneath the cross of Jesus', the tape continued, 'I fain would take my stand, the shadow of a mighty rock within a weary land; a home within the wilderness, a rest upon the way, from the burning of the noontide heat and the burden of the day' (*SASB* 476). I didn't have to carry the burden of confusion – or the burden of my sin – alone.

God's voice reminded me through the next song: 'Not the labours of my hands can fulfil thy law's demands ... thou must save, and thou alone. Nothing in my hand I bring, simply to thy cross I cling; naked, come to thee for dress; helpless, look to thee for grace; foul, I to the fountain fly; Wash me, Saviour, or I die' (*SASB* 302).

This wasn't about me. This wasn't even about my repentance. It was about God's work of grace. And then the promised certainty: 'Blessed assurance, Jesus is mine!' What a gift! All these years later, a shiver runs down my spine as I relive those 15 minutes in the car that day. Was the music a coincidence? Or God's universe in the act of rhyming, as Evelyn Underhill believes?

While sometimes solitude appears as a precious surprise from God, for the most part it has to be planned. As officers we are surrounded by people, so solitude doesn't come easily. My mother found a wall-hanging for me that had numbers that people could take as they queued at my office door, and sometimes I feel like I need them. Our pressing priorities scream from our calendars, and we are driven much of the time by the tyranny of the urgent. But it is possible to plan for solitude, just as we do for a doctor's appointment or a trip to divisional headquarters. It can be scheduled in and treated as a sacred appointment, one that cannot be broken without serious consequences.

SILENCE

During our annual officers' retreat the leader asked us to awaken in silence and maintain that until joining together in a time of worship at 10 am. I loved it. It became a powerful time for me to quieten myself enough to hear the whisper of God. There were some among us who became frustrated. They were so used to noise and people that the silence and the aloneness were difficult to handle. While periods of solitude may include dialogue with the Father or music that carries us toward Heaven, silence plays a large role in bringing us into a spirit of connection with the holy. Even when we are able to stop the noise without, sometimes the noise within is just as loud. So we must find ways to silence the voices, the frivolous thoughts, the list of things undone, so that we might enter into the spirit of the solitary place.

When the 'voices' are a problem, suggests writer Anne Lamott, we should picture holding a jar, above which we hold each of the 'voices' as a mouse by the tail, and drop them into the jar. Then put the lid on, place the jar on a shelf where you can watch the mice scrambling around, squealing away in the confines of the jar – and where, when appropriate, you can lift the lid and listen for a minute or two, but then slam the lid back on and put the jar back on the shelf. At first the silence may be overwhelming but as it becomes more familiar it becomes a welcome companion.

A DAILY JOURNAL

Writing a daily journal has become an essential part of my journey to the centre. Writing allows us to both focus and process, to revisit times of lasting impact and to recognise themes that have been played repeatedly. Write from the outside in, beginning with interactions or events, moving through emotional responses until coming to the essence of feelings and desires – and of God's place in them. Writing a journal condenses thoughts and feelings in order to sift out the extraneous and can clarify what God is doing through the various people and circumstances in life. Write deeply and write with passion, for this discipline is a pathway to the centre.

PRAYER

Prayer is essential in the pursuit of a centredness of soul. It involves types of praying that may appear to be self-centred in its attention, but it is prayer that moves both inward (seeking transformation) and upward (seeking intimacy). Reading slowly and carefully through Richard Foster's *Prayer: Finding the Heart's True Home* is an experience of worship and one of centring in itself, especially in the chapters on the prayer of examen, the prayer of rest, meditative prayer, and contemplative prayer.

THE PRAYER OF EXAMEN

The prayer of examen is an ancient tradition which Foster describes as the examen of consciousness – 'how God has been present to us throughout the day and how we have responded to his loving presence', and the examen of conscience – 'when we uncover those areas that need cleansing, purifying and healing'. In the midst of this praying must be the invitation: 'Lord, show me my sin, show me what there is in my life that comes between us, that keeps me from finding your Spirit as my centre of living. God has been faithful in answering this specific prayer even when I don't really want to hear the answer.

THE PRAYER OF REST

Foster describes the prayer of rest as when 'God places his children in the eye of the storm. When all around us is chaos and confusion, deep within we know stability and serenity.'

'Be still,' says the psalmist. 'Rest,' says the Christ. 'Shalom,' say the Jews. 'Peace I give to you, not as the world gives ...'. It is the Sabbath mindset that Eugene Peterson urges us to: the surrender, the communion, the knowing that when we cannot say a word the spirit groans for us (Romans 8:26). An outcome of our solitary time, the prayer of rest focuses our energy in passionate waiting.

THE PRAYER OF MEDITATION

Meditative prayer can also bring us to a centre. Its closeness to the meditation of the Eastern religions may be a worry, but meditative prayer is what the Scriptures call us to: 'May the words of my mouth and the meditations of my heart be acceptable in thy sight.' I often use Ken Gire's snapshots of biblical encounters in the *Moments with the Saviour* series to aid in meditative prayer, experiencing the fullness of the story and the presence of Christ in my prayer. Meditative prayer awakens the imagination and engages the emotions. I weep with the woman who anointed the feet of Christ, stand back in amazement and awe at the healing of the paralysed man and smile with joy as Jesus takes my child in his arms, as he did the little ones in Judea. I ask: 'What is it you would have me see in this? How can this encounter draw me closer to you? Can I be open to experience your touch, your word to me?'

Foster again is helpful with the concept of the prayer of contemplation, that can 'free us from our addiction to words'. Consider three steps. The first is recollection (the Quaker's 'centring down'), which is a letting go of inner distractions and frustrations. We then can move towards the prayer of quiet.

> *Speak, Lord, in the stillness,*
> *While I wait for thee,*
> *Hushed my heart to listen*
> *In expectancy.*
>
> May Grimes

The recollection and the quiet open us to the work of God in us, the union with his presence, the joy of spiritual ecstasy. Sometimes a fleeting moment, other times a sustained presence, but never of our own making – entirely the work of God in a quiet, receptive

131

heart. It comes not in response to our demand or our pleading, but as grace to our open and vulnerable spirit.

THE PRAYER OF CONTEMPLATION
Experiencing contemplation is not easy. As the Franciscan Richard Rohr tells us: 'We wait in silence. In silence all our usual patterns assault us. Our patterns of control, addiction, negativity, and fear assert themselves ... When Jesus is led by the Spirit into the wilderness, the first things that show up are wild beasts (Mark 1:13) ... As soon as we take away outside stimuli all our inner turmoil erupts – unfinished emotions, unresolved tensions, everyone we want to get angry at, everyone we want to control and change, and all the other things we desire. ... So go into the closet, as Jesus says, and shut the door (Matthew 6:6).'

DISTRACTIONS
In our praying we long to rid ourselves of distractions, the demons which demand our attention throughout the day. The woman who is emotionally and spiritually centred chooses not to surrender to them. The emotional tapes we play back so often, the demands of our jobs, the unrelenting needs of the people we minister to, our hopes and fears, our dreams and our nightmares – all are distractions that keep us from a centre, keep us from the experience of solitude.

Nouwen's description in *Here and Now* is powerful. He pictures a banana tree full of jumping monkeys. I can see them grabbing for bananas, swinging from branches, jockeying for position, all done with a raucous cacophony of sound. We have the ability to exert some control over outward distractions. It's not necessary to keep the mobile phone turned on every hour of every day. It's appropriate sometimes to ask your soldiers to make appointments to talk about serious issues, and we don't have to respond to the email as soon as the message pops up on our screen. Even our children and our husband can learn that an immediate response is not always possible, or in our family's best interest. Patience is one of the fruits of the Spirit and can be taught and modelled.

Distractions are not only external. How often as we pray do our thoughts wander to the next programme we need to plan or the argument we had with our husband that morning? I will be praying and suddenly realise I'm so far away from where I started and where God is, and I have absolutely no idea how I got there! It's easy to be distracted from 'the better things' by a self-imposed perfectionism or the desire to do just one more thing.

Distraction leads us to avoid seriously considering what is going on in our lives. I lamented to a friend about the number of things the Army expected me to do, and how busy that made me, and he asked: 'Are you using all you're doing in the name of ministry to dodge who Christ is calling you to be, to resist looking at your heart?' It's a dilemma for people in ministry, because we are doing good work, we are touching lives, but that work does not excuse us from doing the soulwork within ourselves.

Distraction is a well-used tool of the evil one. Consider the experience of James and John. At a crucial time in the passion of Christ they came with their mother to Jesus and all they wanted to know was where they were going to sit in Jesus' Kingdom (Matthew 20). They were distracted from the reality and pain of the journey by their blinding ambition. I'm no different. I want to talk about my next ministry assignment when God wants my heart. I may need to take a shotgun to the banana tree and chase away a monkey or two if I'm serious about having a life centred on Christ. They may climb back into the tree and squeal all the louder, but I must quieten them down. I must refuse to give the distractions the time and energy they demand if I am to find my way back to the centre.

SIMPLICITY

Another way of reducing distractions is to move towards simplicity in our lives. This theme has figured largely in booksellers' catalogues during the past few years. Sara Ben Breathnach, popular for her writing on simplicity, describes her search: 'Frustrated and unable to fathom why other women appeared to lead much more fulfilling lives – even though I was conscientiously connecting all the dots – I careered between feeling that I was frittering my life away to feeling that I was sacrificing it on the altar of my own ambitions.' Her solution to what felt like an out-of-body existence was a deliberate effort to simplify her life, the basis for much of her writing in recent years.

We are not obliged to have bigger and better, to always come up with another innovative approach to women's ministry or fund-raising. After years of trying to find creative ways of doing the Sunday school Christmas party (and becoming frustrated in the process) I've found the answer for me is to simplify – feed them, share some music and the Word, and pass out the presents.

Simple meals, simple decorations, simple stories and simple programmes make space in my life for the more profound touching of people and communing with God. As I worked in New York following the World Trade Center disaster I found that the technical counselling skills I brought from years of training were surpassed time and again by the simple things: touch, presence, grace. As Quakers know, ''tis a gift to be simple'.

UNREALISTIC EXPECTATIONS

When I was coming of age as a woman, a book travelling the evangelical circuit was Marabel Morgan's *The Total Woman*. It may have been helpful to some, but my reaction was: 'I could never be that woman!' Even at that point in my life I was aware enough to know I couldn't have it all, do it all. A reminder was a picture on the cover of *The Wittenburg Door*, titled 'The Totalled Woman' – a worn down, worn out woman, unkempt, unattractive, soaking her feet in her scrubbing bucket. That picture gave me the courage to accept who I was and what I could do rather than needing to apologise for who I wasn't and what I couldn't do. It brought an awareness that I was not the Total Woman, but neither was I the Totalled Woman – maybe simply a 'Totalling' Woman, one in process.

MAKING IT WORK

What can help in practical ways? Develop an atmosphere of centredness. Consider the sensual surroundings of your office, your home. Find ways to reduce the noise and increase the music. Soften the lighting, light a candle, reduce the glare. Limit the accumulation of 'stuff'. When you need the space, take time out. A nap can bring you back to the place you need to be. Spend some time out of doors each day – and don't count the walk to the car as part of that! Breathing and relaxation exercises can be helpful. An in-service presentation on relaxation walked a group of counsellors through the experience of deep relaxation and it was incredible. I could have spent the rest of the day in that room! It was a deliberate movement toward a mental getaway, a place of warmth, safety and comfort, where it was possible to release the external pressures and distractions and just be. By exerting control over your environment as well as your lifestyle you will create an atmosphere where peace is possible.

RECOGNISE THE FEAR

Some people hesitate to move towards a place of centredness. Consider this question: 'Are you afraid of what you may see?' What if I get away, find a place of solitude and then, nothing. No voice, no comfort, no presence. What if I don't like what I see in myself? What if what God shows me makes me weep – or vomit? Fear is insidious in that it paralyses us in our weakest parts. It, too, is of the evil one. But we have the promise of the Saviour: 'Do not be afraid, little flock, for your Father has been pleased to give you the Kingdom' (Luke 12:32).

GUARDING YOUR HEART

To live from a sense of centredness we must guard our hearts from sin, ever aware of the fragility of our spirit and our inbred bent toward sin. We also must guard our hearts from selfish ambition, the kind that strives for recognition from the world. If our aim in attaining a centredness is to lead others to recognise it and say,

'Oh, what a godly woman she is!' then selfish ambition is the unworthy motivation. And beware of those who will try to strip you of hope. Hope is a marvellous gift of the Spirit, but it can easily be mocked by the evil one. Yet our God is a God of hope, and we must cling to that through the good and bad of life.

THE PLATE-SPINNER

Consider the initial image of this chapter, the juggling plate-spinner. Moving toward a centred life allows our energies to find focus in the juggler (the woman that I am, the spirit of God who dwells within me) rather than in the plates or poles. We have some control over how many poles we pick up, how many hands and feet we use to balance them, and how many plates we spin from day to day. We can start small, by spinning one less plate one day of the week, or it may be that we need to take drastic action and let a number of the twirling discs smash to the ground and shatter.

The Holy One of Israel spoke words of indictment to the Israelites: 'In repentance and rest is your salvation, in quietness and trust is your strength, but you would have none of it' (Isaiah 30:15). Let's claim the promise of the first part of the verse, but not be guilty of its conclusion.

Nine

Where's My Niche?

The impulse to keep to yourself what you have learned is not only shameful; it is destructive. Anything you do not give freely and abundantly becomes lost to you. You open the door of your safe and find ashes.

Annie Dillard

I BEGAN to write songs as a young officer because I needed something to complement my sermon or to use for a special event. Many of my first efforts were used at home league dinners, retreats and camps. My husband suggested a tombstone inscription: 'Here lies JoAnn Shade, home league chorus writer extraordinaire – she has found her niche!' God has led me down alternative paths since those days but a question I have asked repeatedly is: where is my niche? Is there a particular place I belong? Is there a unique contribution I can make to Salvation Army ministry and/or to the Kingdom?

This question was verbalised in a dinner table conversation at the Journey in Grace conference held for officer women in the USA Eastern Territory, about 20 years after my commissioning as an officer. I was seated with four session-mates. All of us were 'midlife' women in our 40s with teenage children or entering the 'empty nest' days. After catching up on family news we reflected on the directions our lives had taken, and how God was at work in us.

Between us we had held a variety of positions within the Army but each of us had discovered the need to find a focus. For some that was graduate work, for others an emphasis on skill-building in a certain area. But for each of us the 'jack-of-all-trades, master-of-none' nature of our early years of officership was becoming a more directed way of living. These choices weren't predicated by the appointments we were serving in but by a realistic evaluation of our gifts and interests and a sharpening of our own desires for impact in the world and the Kingdom. This narrowing of focus was not determined or requested by Salvation Army administration but was a natural development of the work of the Spirit within us.

WOMEN FROM THE WORD: ESTHER

A woman of focus is found in the Book of Esther. While Esther was in a limiting culture for women, she found a niche, a way to speak out at the right time and in the right way to change the course of history for the people of Israel. Esther was a woman who brought a mix of emotions and actions to her role in the drama set forth in that book.

Initially Esther is willing to make the needed preparations for her potential role as queen. The familiar 'beauty shop' scenario shows her interest in making herself pleasing to the king, the easy part of her task. As the story unfolds Esther realises how hazardous her role might be. Her initial reaction is hesitation: 'Not me!' But, after reflection, she comes to the place of saying, 'Why not me?'

Esther was a wise woman, for she realised she could not do what she had to do in her own strength. She determined to do two things: she called upon her people to fast on her behalf, bringing others into the process, and she waited upon God and trusted him to take care of her. In accepting her role she became willing to go to the king on behalf of her people.

Esther was also a woman of courage, trusting her abilities to persuade the king. She did what she had to do to save her people from certain death. Quite a woman, this Esther, and one we can look to as an example for our life of faith.

What can we learn from Esther? There may be a time of preparation that will help to make us 'pleasing' or of greater value to the Movement. We may have second thoughts: 'Should I really be doing this? Maybe someone else could do it?' Spiritual preparation, such as spending time in meditation, fasting or prayer, can make us ready to ask others for assistance in determining our direction. Our niche-seeking must involve trusting God and waiting for his guidance, for we cannot accomplish his work in our own strength. But one day, like Esther, the time comes to step forward with courage and grace, doing what we must, giving ourselves fully to the journey. In time, we will see that we have been prepared 'for such a time as this'.

WHERE DO WE START?

Like Esther, we begin with a time of preparation. As we strive to find our niche, our place in the Army, we can first address the tasks of midlife which allow for a narrowing of focus. Spiritual director Kathleen Fischer describes this transition as 'an experience of personal and social fragmentation that opens the way for a new level of spiritual integration'. Four major areas help us face both the darkness and the dawn.

MIDLIFE TASKS

The first is the opportunity to mourn our losses and limits. Perhaps we've been put on the administrative track and mourn the loss of a congregational ministry. We may have been passed over for a certain position and now know it will never be ours. Our children might disappoint us, or we have regrets about the form our ministry has taken. These losses, as well as other personal grief, can be faced honestly and mourned with the denial, anger, bargaining, depression and acceptance phases that form the pattern of grieving. We also mourn the loss of dreams, the limits that have been placed upon us, the limits we have placed upon ourselves, and the dreams we will never achieve.

The second of Fischer's tasks is to journey inward. We've looked at this in depth in the previous chapter on finding a centre, so I would simply add Anne Morrow Lindbergh's words of encouragement from *Gift from the Sea*: 'One is afraid. Naturally.

Who is not afraid of pure space – that breathtaking empty space of an open door? But, despite fear, one goes through to the room beyond.' The movement inward may seem counter-cultural in an organisation which is so intent on serving others, but, without it, service becomes an empty shell.

Thirdly, midlife is a time to assess our values and life patterns. We can turn off the cruise control and test our convictions, our values and the behaviours which flow from those convictions. Our goal in this is, as Fischer puts it, to 'intensify and simplify our commitments, bringing them more into line with gospel values and the deeper yearnings of our hearts'. What convictions form our foundations for living? Can we articulate them? What do we truly believe about God, people, the world around us? Write them out: 'This is what I believe … .'

Rinehart looked at this from a slightly different perspective by asking himself five questions each day regarding his ministry. I have them framed on my desk, because they prompt me to remember why I am doing what I am doing. While written in a ministry context, they also can be applicable to family, marriage and personal life:

Is Jesus Christ the focus of attention around here?

Are relationships the lifeblood of this ministry?

Can I let go of control and step aside when I need to?

Am I growing more conscious of my convictions, values and assumptions?

What kind of change agent am I?

When I answer these questions honestly I'm brought up short at times and forced to see my sinfulness or disregard for what is right. But at other times I am encouraged by the work God is doing in and through me. Modify these, or write your own, but find a framework to assess your values and behaviour.

Fischer's fourth task is re-balancing the polarities we confront, such as body and spirit, work and play, power and love, youth and age, activity and receptivity, attachment and separateness, destruction and creativity. We can face both the darkness and the light within us without sugar-coating our darkness or minimising our strengths.

Not only can we re-balance, we also can use this time to find ways to be more comfortable with the tension between the polarities. A class I attended on the paradoxes of Christian maturity invited me to wrestle with confusing paradoxes of my faith experience. Why is there both darkness and light in the life of a believer? What can I do when faith and doubt are at war within me? Is there a way to cling to hope in the midst of a time of despair? Life is difficult, and we will struggle in many ways. When we acknowledge that tension we can minimize our surprise or disappointment when adversity strikes.

The underlying theme of Fischer's tasks speaks to a finding of self. When we know who we are – with our strengths and weaknesses, our likes and dislikes, our areas of temptation and the presence of God within us – we can move outward in a healthy and holy direction.

AMBITION

How does a woman officer come to grips with ambition? As a young woman, did Esther dream of being one of the king's wives? When the opportunity came to her, some probably labelled her ambitious or aspiring, but look at the loss to her people if she had said no. 'I have an ambition. I truly have a desire to achieve.' In a culture of service to others this sounds so worldly, so un-submissive, so un-Christian. Where does the drive for effectiveness, a passion for ministry or a desire to provide leadership in a Movement to which we are committed cross the line to sinful, self-serving ambition?

Is that a gender-defined line within the Army? Is it appropriate for a woman (single or married) to desire – and work towards – a leadership appointment? William Booth wrote: 'Women shall have the right to an equal share with men in the work of publishing salvation. A woman may hold any position of power and authority within the Army. Women must be treated as equal with men in all intellectual and social relationships of life.'

General John Gowans (as he later became) commented on this subject a number of years ago in *The Officer*, declaring: 'There should be no need for our Army women to make such a claim [as Icelandic women did for recognition and important posts in leadership] because the opportunities ought to be theirs as of right, an inherent right that has been part of the Army's distinctiveness since its beginning and which was achieved by the founding Mother of the Army, Catherine Booth. However, the question needs to be asked (and answered), "Does the Army of the 80s give less or more leadership opportunities for women officers?"'

Commissioner Marjorie Hodder, on her installation as National President of Women's Organisations in the USA in 1993, stated that her goal was to 'promote vigorously and successfully William Booth's vision of women officers admitted to full participation in the government of The Salvation Army'. General Gowans returned to the same subject in his statement on officership in 2000, supporting the International Commission on Officership's recommendations; declaring that women officers should be appointed to positions commensurate with their gifts and experience, and that there should be a gender balance in the membership of planning and decision-making bodies.

FINDING YOUR WAY

While history and current regulation would indicate that leadership opportunities are available regardless of gender, many women officers recognise that what exists on paper doesn't necessarily exist in practice. One of the initial struggles for a woman called and equipped for leadership is to determine how to access that opportunity. Like Esther, we often must find our own way through this. When Esther was in the harem she had to sink or swim. While there are new winds blowing today, other than in exceptional cases the Army does not decide a particular focus or ministry path for most women officers. Still the aura of dependency built into the Army structure does not openly encourage the kind of independent thinking that says, 'This is who I am, this is what I want – and am called – to do.'

Miriam Adeney, writing about women and the Church, suggests: 'When an organisation is stretching, every worker counts. But when an organisation is consolidating, women become decorative assistants.' My reading of Salvation Army history tells me there was definitely a drawing back from the very early days of women in leadership, as the Movement became routinised and more bureaucratic. A while ago, reading some *Officer* articles on the family, I was struck by how many high-ranking female officers (married) spoke of having to find their own ministry many times during their officership, as they weren't specifically given assignments which utilised their gifts in an effective way. As I finished reading I wept, thinking of the lost opportunity the Army had in those situations, as well as the message that pattern sends to young women in this ministry.

Observing the history of women's roles in *What's Holding You Back?*, Linda Austin suggests that 'active, aggressive identification of problems to tackle is a radically new role for women in history. Our traditional role has always been to fix the problems that were assigned to us, both at home and in the workplace. As a group, women simply must become more active in finding our own great problems to solve if we are to take our place as thought leaders and visionaries. Often there are many opportunities for growth and development, and considerable flexibility given to [married] women officers, yet those opportunities aren't going to seek us out. We must ask for what we want and need, and build a case for participation that is a logical one.'

Major Libbet Booth wrote in *The Officer*: 'Because of my own experience I believe everyone has something the Lord wants to use. In fact it is because of that something that he chose us. Originally the Army was bursting with individuals, all doing their own thing, as it were, but as so often happens to organisations with growth and the passing of time, it has become settled, with an accepted idea of what is the norm of behaviour and service. There is, of course, both good and bad in this. For some, belonging to the Army organisation works. It nourishes and brings out their particular gift. But in other cases it does not. There is little point in blaming the organisation, the onus to do something about it is on the individual. We are still accountable for our gifts, I believe, whether the Army can use them or not.'

VALUABLE TO THE ARMY ... AND THE KINGDOM

How can I make myself valuable to the Movement? Brainstorm the possibilities, such as gaining advanced mediation skills in preparation for resolving marital or congregational disputes, or training in domestic violence or sexual abuse prevention and treatment to provide needed advocacy and counsel. It may take time, but you are building a reputation as one who can be contacted when that need presents itself. You may not consider yourself an expert but you will have a library of knowledge and experience, both literally and figuratively, that can be a useful resource to other officers.

PRACTICAL IMPLICATIONS

Where do you see gaps within what we do as a movement? If a gap fits your interests and abilities, go for it! At worst you will be of increased effectiveness to your local ministry but at best you will make a lasting contribution through the worldwide ministry of the Army and in the structure of the Movement, so that those following you will have richer support in their work.

I know this takes time. It takes time to do the work of knowing yourself and finding your niche. It takes time to develop the particular gifts that will nurture your ability to occupy that niche. It takes time for the work to bear fruit, as education or training is needed to perform adequately in a given role. This is time that must be taken away from family, corps and practical ministry in the short term, in order to accomplish a long-term goal. It's not an easy choice.

But midlife does bring a different sense of time, in that we are no longer tied to childcare routines. We can also appreciate the concept of delayed gratification. I liken this time to that of pregnancy. The nine months of pregnancy are a waiting time and a season of preparation. When the time has come, the birth occurs and the child arrives. Sacrifices of time during early midlife prepares for the birth of a new focus, a distinctive niche that will bless many people in the future, and fully utilise your gifts. Yes, further education courses, postgraduate studies or intensive training is tough – staying up late finishing papers and spinning an extra plate or two for a period of time; but the skills and character developed through that time can be life-changing.

COMMITMENT

What of commitment? Am I willing to make the hard choices necessary to achieve what I desire? We readily understand that to become a physician, a student must have a solid commitment to their goal in order to accept the staggering hours and hard work required. As an officer, the end result is not as tangible as a medical degree – there's no guarantee of a new position or different responsibilities, and no financial incentives – so an intrinsic motivation is needed to persevere.

STOP AND LOOK

Am I content to plod along as a mediocre officer, or am I willing to do what it takes to sharpen my skills and become a competent, proficient officer who has a particular speciality?

We have the opportunity at midlife to have input over the direction of the rest of our life, even though life at this stage may still seem like a runaway train as it did for Christian writer Paula D'Arcy: 'Now I begin to review the past four or five years of my life. The truth wounds my pride. I see that since my whole career of writing and public speaking began there was never a moment when I consciously decided this was the path I should follow. Nor did I ever ask God, "Is this the way you want me to go?" I made a lot of assumptions. It was Christian ministry, so of course it was good. I never asked the question, but is it right for *me*? Is it right *at this time*? Right *at this pace*? I see how prone I am to run headlong into people's needs. But by living in this way, I give away pieces of my life. Important pieces. Pieces of my energy, my time, my strength. On the basis of assumptions (this *must* be right) as opposed to intentions (I *choose* to go this way), I have given over ownership of me.'

In the spirit of Frederick Buechner's words on calling, Ken Gire invites us to 'look back on your life and put frames around the things that brought you joy'. In the framing we can accept that it is OK to 'listen to the voices of our own gladness'.

PRIDE AND HUMILITY

What if you develop a speciality and nobody notices? It opens up the question of pride versus humility. During my counselling internship I travelled a long distance to be part of a practice that would stretch me through its supervision and training. Clients would cancel and I would end up seeing one person in an evening. One night, as I was whining to myself about how little I was being used, it struck me – this wasn't about me. If God had called me to this because of the one client I saw that night, that's what he called me to do. Jesus reminds us in the parable of the talents (Matthew 25:14-30) that it is important to be faithful in using what he has given us, and that when we are faithful in the small things he will entrust us with more in his Kingdom.

THE MOMMY TRACK

Women in corporate America are familiar with what's been dubbed 'the mommy track'. Officers who happen to be mothers often have a great deal of flexibility in what they do within the Army, and, unlike corporate America, there is no financial penalty required of those who choose the full-time mommy track. Within the team ministry concept, the mommy track option doesn't generally affect adversely the career development of an officer couple. Where it may be of issue is when the woman comes to a place where she wants to become more fully involved in the corporate leadership of the Army, but is perceived as being still on the mommy track. Even when that desire is specifically articulated, it may take a while for those perceptions to be changed within the administration.

STAINED-GLASS CEILING

What about the glass ceiling? The 'stained-glass ceiling' is a term that has been coined to describe the limits placed on women in the Church. While, on paper, the stained-glass ceiling should not exist within the Army, a cursory glance through the disposition of forces indicates that it is alive and well.

What can be done about it? I see four options. The first is to be resigned to the fact that it exists: 'I know I won't get past that stained-glass ceiling, so there's no sense in trying.' The second is to be totally frustrated by it and either complain about your lot in life or find affirmation and growth elsewhere. A third option calls us to face it head on, speaking directly to the injustice and demand that change occur. A fourth option comes from an image Christian psychologist Dan Allender used in a seminar to describe an effective therapist. He asked: 'Have you ever seen a cockroach that couldn't get where he/she wanted to go?'

A good therapist will be like that cockroach. He or she will somehow find a way to get to a person's heart. If you, as a committed, well-equipped Army officer, desire to minister in a particular way, there are means to get to that place. It may be through the front door, prising open a window or crawling up the ductwork, but persistence and a clear focus will get you where God needs you to be, one way or another.

Elements of the four options may be useful at various times, but a guiding principle is the question: what kind of Army do I hope to leave to the next generation of women, and what part can I have in creating that Army?

NEW MAPS

This journey may involve seeking out new maps. Joyce Rupp speaks of it this way: 'Midlife has been a continual process of getting terribly lost inside, feeling far away from who I am, from the space of "me", struggling and yearning to come home to myself and then, all of a sudden, feeling at home, finding a space in me that I had either forgotten or newly discovered.'

New maps allow us to question what we have been following and why, and we begin the process of sorting out what is truly biblical and what we've been conditioned to accept. We listen to the stirrings in our mind and heart, and trust ourselves to be open to the Holy Spirit's whispers and nudges.

What if following the new map leads you away from the Army? As a Catholic nun, Rupp faced the same kind of question: 'There were times when I was ready to step off the well-worn road, to toss the old map away, but I feared making unwise decisions about the future. I remember a section of my midlife passage when I grew very doubtful about my vowed life in my religious community. The vows of celibacy, poverty and obedience, which I had promised 25 years earlier, no longer seemed adequate. The outdated structures had changed but the old vision, based on a parent-child mode of relating, was deeply rooted. While I struggled and stumbled around in my questions and my doubts, I also sought the help of a wise companion ... Instead of urging me to leave my community she invited me to dream of a religious community the way I would envision it. What would it look like? What would give my vows meaning and substance? What would help me be psychologically and spiritually healthy? Was leaving my community the only option or was there a way for me to remain faithful but also be true to the growth that was occurring for me?'

Her questions are appropriate for us. Are there ways to remain faithful but also true to the growth we are experiencing? Obviously, the implications of leaving the safety and familiarity of the Army are huge. Financially it is difficult to walk away from the benefits provided, as well as from the promised retirement provision. If you are married, your husband may or may not share your sense of 'new maps', which can put considerable strain on the marriage relationship. In the USA it is still not

148

possible for one spouse to leave officership while the other remains an active officer, so any thought of seeking a new vocational path directly affects the spouse. In the context of a lifelong call, the strains of 'I cannot leave the dear old flag, 'twere better far to die' tend to float through my head when thoughts of leaving officership come up.

WHAT KIND OF NICHE?

If your new maps direct you to remain faithful but also true to the growth that is calling you, the development of a niche in ministry will support that growth. There are many possibilities and exploring these ideas can be fun. What are you already doing that draws you and awakens your passion? What do you look forward to most in your week? Is there something in your current work that others see as an area of giftedness? These are clues to your niche.

A young friend told me, 'I want to live so that when I get to Heaven I don't have regrets about how I used the gifts given to me.' She knew that, for her, it meant she must sing more and teach more. On reading her words, what do *you* think of first? 'I must ...'

It may be there is something new awaiting your exploration. Perhaps you see needs within your ministry that you truly want to meet, but don't have the skills to do that well. Maybe there is something you have never tried, but it is calling your name. That prompting may be of the Holy Spirit, moving you forward through the face of need. I'll borrow an image from Chris Fabray (*At the Corner of Mundane and Grace*): 'I want to live now in a way that when I'm old and grey, sitting on the porch in my rocking chair, with nothing left but my gums and my memories, I'll be OK with my choices.'

PREACHING

Here are a few ideas. As already observed, effective preaching is a niche that has regular benefit to the Movement, the congregation and other women. Can you envision yourself as a more effective communicator? Start following that thread – spend more time in sermon preparation, read in that area, take a course at a Bible college or seminary – and see where it leads you.

TEACHING

You may be gifted in teaching and want to pursue that role. You can teach in areas you are already competent in, or you may need to develop a specialisation in knowledge before you can teach from that storehouse. Who is an expert within the Army on Church history, Army history, child development, sexual abuse or crisis counselling? Some have pursued a specific field deliberately, while others have fallen into it, but they are the ones who are called upon to teach when needed, and consulted for advice when appropriate, even if their particular appointment continues to be a mainstream one.

THEOLOGY

One discipline that women are noticeably absent from within Army circles is that of theology. I was struck by this gap in reading an article by General John Larsson in *Word and Deed*, when he wrote of the Army's theologians of note, from the early era to today. Of the 18 names he listed, only one was a woman – Catherine Booth, who died more than 100 years ago. Shame on us, as women, for not stepping up to the plate theologically! And shame on the Movement for its practices that do not encourage female theological development!

WOMEN'S SPIRITUAL DEVELOPMENT

Another area which, to my knowledge, has found little attention within Army circles is women's spiritual development. With all the resources we expend on women's ministries we speak very little about the way in which women come to faith and mature spiritually. Perhaps our hesitation comes because much of this study focuses on feminist theology, which at times becomes quite strident and threatening. But this is another niche in which there is plenty of room for women who are drawn to this type of study and exploration.

COUNSELLING

As a corps officer I often faced situations that were beyond my ability to handle. Yet I knew that our people had little or no opportunity to find biblical counselling for their issues and I longed to touch their pain and bring healing through the power of Christ in a caring and competent way. When I ultimately sought out graduate studies, this was the direction I chose, and while I can now function more effectively and appropriately in counselling situations the education has also broadened other interests for me as well.

ADMINISTRATIVE ROLES

Given the dual ministry role, it has been difficult for married women to assume high-powered administrative roles within the Army. It is also a role that may not be easily accepted by others in leadership. It may be, however, that this is a niche that fits for you. As Dr Lucille G. Ford, an economist, educator and author, reminds us, while it is possible to move in the business workplace, 'it was [is] a lonely road ... I forced myself, by choice and by requirement, to keep my mind focused on my mission'. New winds are now blowing, so if administration is your gift, go for it!

NURTURING

Some women come to officership with a real love for children. This, too, can be a niche that reaps great results. There are countless stories of children being virtually adopted by officers, bringing a life-giving sense of stability to their lives. Homes that are open and welcoming to teenagers and young adults can be a blessed haven in the midst of chaos. The gift of hospitality is a wonderful treasure to share and can have a lasting impact on many.

CREATIVITY

As we move from task-oriented functions to more creative or intuitive ones we find that women do not fare much better in this arena. While there are many talented musicians within the Army who are female, the majority of published music is written by males. The same is true of literature. Glancing at the bookshelves of Army authors during recent Old Orchard camp meetings I was saddened to note a one-in-ten ratio of female-to-male authors. Those barren bookshelves were an impetus to me to get more serious about writing, if only to shift the ratio a bit more toward a gender balance. Women must make the effort to write and to submit their work for publication. They must believe enough in their efforts to want them to be available to others, and to work to make that happen.

Do we need some affirmative action here? How can all forms of artistic expression be supported? Janet Luhrs challenges us: 'Creativity means opening your box, tearing down the sides and stretching out to discover new ways of looking at and doing things that will improve your life.'

To be fair, this phenomenom is not unique to the Army. James Terry explores the place of women in the arts through history and recognises the dearth of female musicians and artists through the centuries. In considering the reasons, he suggests societal acceptance, not lack of talent or ability, tended to keep women from being known as artists. He writes that, for the aristocracy, 'the demands of their social class did not allow them time for serious development of creative talents. Exactly the same holds true for women.' He challenges us with this statement: 'The question of how much creative talent has been stifled because of society's sexual bias should haunt us.'

CONTEMPLATION
A final niche for this chapter is one not encountered very often among Salvationists, perhaps due to the very pragmatic nature of the Army. It is the role of mystic. There is an aspect to Catherine Booth's writings that speaks to the contemplative, but in recent years much emphasis has been upon doing rather than being. Perhaps it is time for a woman or two of this century to follow her heart to the inner recesses of mysticism. Are there other possibilities? Of course – that is the uniqueness of Army ministry

and 21st-century potential. It is up to us to be open to the creative, sanctified imagination that is available to each of us.

HOW DO YOU DECIDE?

My initial search for a niche brought me up against the realisation that I was quite eclectic by nature, and finding one particular focus was not necessarily going to happen for me. I felt a bit like Winnie the Pooh in *House at Pooh Corner*:

'"What do you like doing best in the world, Pooh?" "Well," said Pooh, "what I like best ..." And then he had to stop and think. Because although Eating Honey *was* a very good thing to do, there was a moment just before you began to eat it which was better than when you were, but he didn't know what it was called. And then he thought that being with Christopher Robin was a very good thing to do, and having Piglet near was a very friendly thing to have; and so, when he had thought it all out, he said, "What I like best in the whole world is Me and Piglet going to see You, and You saying, 'What about a little something?' and Me saying, 'Well, I shouldn't mind a little something, should you, Piglet?' and it being a hummy sort of day outside, and the birds singing."'

Perhaps your niche will be that of a renaissance woman, accomplished in a variety of areas, but one still able to hear the birds singing. It is your choice to make in living out your God-given calling to ministry and faith.

To get there, begin by exploring. Take a class or two, try some new things, write a song or get out the pastels or oils. Follow your gifts. Take a spiritual gifts inventory, explore the Myers-Briggs Personality Inventory, try out the Holland career model or check out *What Color Is Your Parachute?* (Richard Nelson Bolles) – a helpful career exploration. Seek guidance from trusted friends who know you well. Consider how God has made things clear to you in the past – through meditation, fasting, solitude, counsel – and seek that out. Above all, be sensitive to the Spirit's wooing through this time, for 'He who began a good work in you will be faithful to complete it'. Most of all, do not be afraid to look for your niche. As

Thomas Merton reminds us: 'Our vocation is not simply to be, but to work together with God in the creation of our own life, our own identity, our own destiny.'

BALANCE

A secular book on feminine leadership development, *What's Holding You Back?*, puts the pieces together for us: 'The goal is to live a life that reflects a balanced sense of meaning, allowing for a free range of choices and creative problem-solving that begins with the assumption that it is possible both to love and to work without feeling like a martyr in the process. Developing such a value system involves both clarifying and developing a sense of meaning that honours both love and self.'

We can, indeed, love – both God and each other – and honour our own personality and interests in the ministry by finding a niche of our own. For too long, at least some women within the Army have been like the man who received one talent but buried it because he was afraid. We have a choice: we can discover what God has gifted us to and move in that direction, or we can bury it. As Deborah Flagg reminds us: 'When God-given gifts go unused, the whole body is impoverished. Gifts that are used bring opportunities for grace.' For with the discovery of our gifts comes the responsibility to use them well, as Lareta Halerman Finger understands: 'The identifying of gifts brings to the fore ... the issue of commitment. Somehow, if I name my gift and it is confirmed, I cannot "hang loose" in the same way. I would much rather be committed to God in the abstract than to be committed to him at the point of my gifts ... Commitments at the point of my gifts means that I must give up being a straddler ... Life will not be the smorgasbord I have made it, sampling and tasting here and there. My commitment will give me an identity.'

Like Esther, it may be we are being prepared 'for such a time as this', and it is up to us to move with trust in God's direction and recognition of our own courage, investing our talents in a way that will truly bless others.

Ten

Connections

Who else but a woman listens with sympathetic nods,
wraps us up in a woolly afghan, fixes us lunch,
bakes our favourite cookies, and makes us a bottomless cup of tea?
Our best friends are part mother, sister, saint;
they know our souls and love us into our strengths and despite
our weaknesses.

Holly Larsen

AS I read Holly Larsen's words, they take me back more than 10 years, when reading these words brought me to tears. Larry and I had spent five years in a demanding inner-city appointment, and I came to the end of that time with the recognition that there really wasn't anybody in my life like the person Holly describes. There was no woman I prayed with on a regular basis, no woman who held me accountable for my family and ministry, no woman to whom I could confess my sin, no woman who could accept my tears or share my joy at any depth – not even a woman I could just hang out with. I don't believe it was intentional – after all, I was around lots of people every day, I was absorbed in a difficult but rewarding ministry, I was involved with my children and husband, I had a few friends within the Army, and life was going on – but as I look back honestly, I was extremely isolated. By nature I tend to be a private person. But as I pondered where I was and where I was going, I resolved that I was no longer willing to live life in such a lonely way.

At that time, I was reading Lewis Smedes's *Caring and Commitment,* which described so well what I needed to find: 'The trick is to find a real community, not an insider's club. Not a group that makes believe it is a community, just because everyone recites the same creed. But a community where people care enough to give each other permission to be strugglers, wounded strugglers, who are hanging on to their commitments by their fingernails. A community that cares enough to permit people to fail helps people dare to reveal their own struggles, including their failures as well as successes.'

I wrote those words in my journal and made them my prayer: 'Lord, help me to find that sense of community in my life; let me make myself vulnerable to others so that they will know my heart – and I will know theirs.' God was extremely gracious to me in bringing people into my life that became community for me – scattered though we were, and limited though our time together sometimes was.

BUILT FOR RELATIONSHIP
Recent writings and studies on the subject of the differences between male and female have echoed the theme that women are more relationally connected than men. The popular *Men are from Mars, Women are from Venus* series points this out clearly. Jean Baker Miller writes: 'Women's sense of self becomes very much organised around being able to make and then to maintain affiliations and relationships. We all begin life deeply attached to the people around us. Men, or boys, are encouraged to move out of this state of existence in which they and their fate are intimately intertwined in the lives and fate of other people. Women are encouraged to remain in this state, but, as they grow, to transfer their attachment to a male figure.'

Singer Barbra Streisand was right in her basic assumption: 'People who need people are the luckiest [most blessed!] people in the world.' This desire and need for relationships is not wrong and does not inevitably lead to co-dependence. It is a natural strength of women, and Miller encourages women to 'choose relationships that foster mutual growth'.

156

Researcher Carol Gilligan also addresses the belief that women approach life differently to men, describing the female approach as: 'Identity is defined in the context of relationship.' Crabb suggests: 'A woman is less centrally focused on achievement as a means for feeling complete ... more, she tends to value giving something of herself to nourish relationships and deepen attachments. Her focus is less on going into the world and more on entering a relational network.' We women are designed to be relational, and when that design is ignored we wake up one morning alone and weep, unless we have numbed ourselves so much as to be dead inside.

WOMEN FROM THE WORD

Can you imagine sneaking a look into the Bethlehem stable, or watching from the shadows as Jesus intervened in the stoning of a woman, or being caught up in the Palm Sunday euphoria? What an experience, to have been one of the women who travelled with Jesus! They always seemed to be together. They show up from time to time, these named and unnamed women who ministered to Jesus. In the 10 times these women were mentioned in the Gospels, only once was a woman alone (Mary Magdalene at the tomb in John 21). On every other occasion they were side by side. Just as women today need each other, it would appear that these women of the Gospels, who had the privilege of serving their servant Lord Jesus, did so as women together in relationship.

We have minimal information about them. Some were named, such as Mary Magdalene, Salome, Mary the mother of James, and Joses the mother of Zebedee's sons, Mary the wife of Clopas, Joanna the wife of Cuza, Susanna, and Mary the mother of Jesus. Others were anonymous, unnamed for history, but known to each other – and to Jesus.

It appears that whatever these women did, they did in a group, perhaps as encouraged by the culture of their day. We see first that they served together. Luke 8 tells us that the 12 disciples were with Jesus, and also some women who had been cured of evil spirits and diseases: Mary (called Magdalene); Joanna the wife of Cuza, the manager of Herod's household; Susanna; and many others. These women were helping to support them out of their own means. Matthew 27:55 (*TNIV*) tells us, 'They had followed Jesus from Galilee to care for his needs.'

'To care for his needs' was not a small task. It is likely that they arranged for housing for Jesus and the 12 named disciples, as well as 'the many others'. There were meals to cook (with no local supermarkets) or arrange, water to carry and clothing to wash and mend. Perhaps one or two of them moved ahead of the group, smoothing the way for the disciples through the contacts they had in the various villages.

As Jesus moved toward the culmination of his journey to the cross, these same women watched together. Matthew 27:55 tells us that 'many women were there [at the cross], watching from a distance'. Among them were Mary Magdalene, Mary the mother of James and Joses, and the mother of Zebedee's sons. Mark 15:40 tells us: 'Some women were watching from a distance. Among them were Mary Magdalene,' while John 19:25 reports: 'Near the cross of Jesus stood his mother, his mother's sister, Mary the wife of Clopas, and Mary Magdalene' (*NIV*).

These women also mourned together: 'A large number of people followed him, including women who mourned and wailed' (Luke 23:27). Picture them huddled together, holding hands or leaning on each other, 'keening' – an eerie wailing sound that spills unchecked from the very depths of a person. As they mourned, they waited together. Luke 23:55, 56 (*NIV*) tells us: 'The women who had come with Jesus from Galilee followed Joseph and saw the tomb and how his body was laid in it. Then they went home and prepared spices and perfumes.'

They were also witnesses to the resurrection together. We find an assortment of women at the tomb: Luke places Mary Magdalene and the other Mary, Joanna and others there, hearing the report of the angel and seeing the empty tomb. Matthew reports that Mary and Mary Magdalene were there. Mark adds Salome to the group, while John speaks only of Mary (although her use of the word 'we' (John 20:2) suggests someone else with her, and John's snapshot of the encounter between Jesus and Mary allows for the possibility that others may have been there before or after. They saw what they saw and then went to tell, having their witness questioned by the disciples.

Their relationship was not described in detail but it is likely that in the midst of their work (serving, watching, mourning, waiting, anointing, witnessing) they came to know each other well and to value the sisterhood they shared. When godly women spend time together, either in work or in waiting, they move towards each other in their faith, and I imagine these biblical women used much of their time together to pray and share in spiritual conversation. We have the opportunity to be their sisters in our relationships with others, if we claim the courage to do so.

THE DANGER OF ISOLATION

While we may desire to have connected relationships we are hampered in coming together by the fact that life in church leadership is, by its nature, isolated. We've heard the cautions: 'Don't get too close to the people in the corps. Don't let them call you by your first name. You know that you can't, by regulation, stay in contact once you leave, so why get close now? You may need to discipline them in some way, you might get entangled with their stuff, remember your boundaries.' There is wisdom in using care in developing relationships within the congregation but if we are serious about inviting community there must be a willingness on our part to offer ourselves to those we worship with. We cannot allow the structure to keep us from developing deep mutual relationships.

Women who nurture close relationships with other women are healthier in their souls. They are better able to see their own foolishness and sin, as well as to be encouraged in their ministry and family life. Having experienced wonderful friendships over the past few years I couldn't imagine going back to the place where I had been, in that painful, self-imposed isolation. I am so blessed to have friends who are as those described by Benedict Groeschel: 'When the dark recesses of our spirit become manifest, we especially need at least a friend to share our fears and assure us that ours is not an uncommon experience.'

LOYALTY, CARE AND CLAIM

Lewis Smedes describes committed friendship in three ways. First, committed friends are loyal. 'Loyalty,' he says, 'is the consistency that gives friendship a toughness to survive when it costs a person something to stick with a friend.' It is also about caring: 'If I care for you as my friend, whatever happens to you happens to me; when sadness hits you it hits me too; when tragedy wallops you, it wallops me; when something terrific happens to you, I celebrate no matter where I happen to be.' Thirdly, friendship is about accepting a friend's claim on us. We spend time with them, come to their rescue, bake their favourite kind of cookie or babysit when they're in a bind, just because. We belong together.

'Piglet sidled up to Pooh from behind. "Pooh," he whispered. "Yes, Piglet?" "Nothing," said Piglet, taking Pooh's paw. "I just wanted to be sure of you."'

OBJECTIONS

I hear the objections starting. I know what they are, because I have used them all: 'I don't really need anybody like that. I do OK on my own. I don't have time. My corps just doesn't have anybody in it I connect with. I don't know how to meet people I can have that kind of relationship with. I can't trust anyone in the Army. I don't think I can risk it. If I develop those kinds of friendships, it will hurt too much to dig up the roots when we have to move.' Let's look at them one by one, and debunk the myths involved.

WE NEED EACH OTHER

First, the belief that as women we can get along without friends is bogus. Ruth Senter reminds us: 'It is fantasy to believe we will always be strong. Even the strongest among us will some day face something that will cause us to wilt like a daisy in the sun. Sooner or later, something will drain the self-assuredness right out of our veins. Then what?'

Ruth Josselson, writing in *Finding Herself*, puts it in a different light: 'Male development is hierarchical, like a pyramid. Throughout their lives, men are concerned with ascendancy and self-protection in conversation and life. Female development, on the other hand, is interconnected like a web. Women disclose, making themselves vulnerable in order to anchor their lives in relationships with men, children, and other women.'

We may think we can go it alone, and may be able to for a time, but we really do need each other as women of God.

TIME

'I don't have time.' I've said it, too. While I was at Cleveland Hough I thought I just didn't have time for working on relationships, there was always so much to do. But I paid dearly for that misguided decision. If I had been less isolated I would have been more effective in my ministry – that was the bottom line, and I didn't come to realise it until it was time to leave that appointment. Developing and maintaining friendships of worth is time-consuming. There is no getting around that. I probably set aside, on average, two hours a week for this, which has now become an absolute lifeline to me. It may involve phone calls, lunch, or late night coffee but it is time that is essential to me.

If you seriously believe you cannot spare two hours out of the week's total of 168 (which is just 1.2 per cent of your time) I urge you to consider what else you may be giving two hours a week to – television, a manicure, reading, work at the corps that someone else could possibly do – and ask whether that activity takes the place of what connection with another believer can bring to your heart and mind. By all means keep in touch through email, cards, phone calls – even long-distance relationships can be enriching.

161

NOBODY HOME

'I don't connect with anyone in the corps.' This may be true. I'm not suggesting you will always find the kind of soulmate you desire within the local congregation, and when you do there are certain limitations on that friendship that need to be considered. Dual relationship is the term used in counsellor training to caution the therapist against having a relationship outside the counselling office when there is an unequal power differential in the relationship, or supervisory responsibilities over someone else. The dilemma is that if we truly desire our people to develop true community with each other then we cannot hold ourselves aloof from them. We must find our own way through the relational maze, but a Christ-honouring love is one that is not shared from 'above' but one that comes alongside. The postmodern Church faces a new paradigm in that it is primarily relational in nature, and that must include the officer/pastor.

The wisdom of Isaiah 54:2 rings true: 'Enlarge the place of your tent, stretch your tent curtains wide, do not hold back; lengthen your cords, strengthen your stakes' (*TNIV*). It may be necessary to widen your circle of acquaintants in your community to find a soulmate. You may find that friend in a ministerial association, a young mothers' group, Babysong, an advisory board member or spouse, a classmate on a continuing education course or a support group. She might be your hairdresser, your child's teacher or the mother of a friend of your child. She may be a fellow officer who is just as hungry for relationship, or an employee at the corps or headquarters.

While this relational concept is helpful in friendship evangelism we need at least one person in our life who shares our faith experience, so keep looking until you find someone who clicks with your spiritual needs, interests and experience. Having one, deep spiritual friendship certainly doesn't limit other relationships of depth – in fact it will enhance those as you gain the ability to trust and to strip off the layers of masks we all too often wear.

I DON'T KNOW HOW

'I don't know how to connect with people I can have that kind of relationship with.' The secret is to start where you're at, looking around at who you know, and being deliberate and intentional in pursuing a relationship with someone. Be alert when you gather with other women. Perhaps you will hear another talk about a favourite author of yours, or a mutual friend you share. Eleanor Roosevelt had it right: 'If you approach each new person you meet in a spirit of adventure, you will find yourself endlessly fascinated by the new channels of thought and experience and personality that you encounter.' Train yourself to be curious about another person, and listen for cues that say, 'I am a woman who is seeking after God's heart.' Then go ahead and ask. Say something like: 'I feel as though we have a lot in common. I wonder if we could get together for lunch some day to get to know each other better.' And suggest a time and place. At some point it is important and respectful to the other woman to articulate what you want: someone to pray with once a week; a mentor or spiritual director; someone to talk with about the deepest issues of life and faith; or just a friend to be goofy with!

'I can't trust anyone in the Army.' A sad statement but true for some. There are legitimate reasons to use care within our ministry hierarchy in developing relationships of depth. Dual relationships is one reason, as is the reputation some Salvationists have for gossip. Yet what is the Army? Is it truly the Body of Christ? If so, we cannot abdicate our responsibility to both seek out and offer godly relationships. Choose wisely, and if you feel uneasy about a relationship, trust your feelings and use care in what you say and where you go with it. Make that a topic of conversation: 'I'm feeling awkward about what we've just talked about. I think maybe I shouldn't have said what I did. How is it making you feel?' Talk about confidentiality: what is said here stays here, unless you give me permission to share it with another.

Don't be afraid to go outside the Army to develop these kinds of relationships. Three of my dearest friends have absolutely no connection with The Salvation Army, and that offers an unbiased arena to sort out concerns without any risk of repercussions. We can get so tied up within the culture of the Movement that we live in a Salvationist ghetto, similar to the ethnic ghettos in many European countries prior to the Second World War. It's refreshing to have friendships where I have no rank, no identity other than JoAnn, and we can simply be two women, coming together in Christ, with no organisational agenda.

RISK

'I don't think I can risk it.' Friendship of this nature is a risky business. You can get hurt. You can hurt the other person. C. S. Lewis reminds us: 'To love at all is to be vulnerable. Love anything, and your heart will certainly be wrung and possibly be broken. If you want to make sure of keeping it intact, you must give your heart to no one ... wrap it carefully with hobbies and little luxuries, avoid all entanglements, lock it up safe in a casket ... of your own selfishness ... there it will not be broken; it will become unbreakable, impenetrable, irredeemable.'

What do you want from relationships in your life? Dina Craik's words awaken a hunger in me: 'Oh, the comfort – the inexpressible comfort of feeling safe with a person, having neither to weigh thought nor measure words but pouring them all out, just as they are – chaff and grain together – certain that a faithful hand will take and sift them, keep what is worth keeping and with the breath of kindness blow the rest away.'

Franciscan Richard Rohr writes: 'The risk, fear and discipline involved in loving rightly cause people to use religion to avoid the tremendous amount of darkness and suffering that goes into the mature development of any human relationship.' In deep relationships we are called to enter the darkness, to suffer alongside our friends. It's risky but sacred business.

What of relationships gone sour? Ruth Senter experienced that: 'You pay. You pay dearly. Sometimes, in the aftermath, resentment builds. Used. Disposed. Like a crumpled paper cup that no longer

164

holds water. You write "Going Out of Business" across the Good Samaritan that is in you, and you keep yourself on the far side – the safe side – of the Jericho road.' Perhaps this has been your experience, but you want to try again. Recognise what went wrong and assume the blame that rightfully belongs to you. Process that reaction, and as you develop a new relationship or deepen an existing one be open about your past experience and how it is affecting the current relationship.

GOODBYES

'It will hurt too much to dig up the roots when we have to move.' Ah, yes, it will. We are back to the Velveteen Rabbit issues. In this day of enhanced communication methods, relocation does not necessarily have to end friendships, but they surely become more difficult to maintain. When I first penned these words, a while ago, I couldn't speak from experience because I was in the midst of what turned out to be a nine-year corps appointment marked by deep-rooted friendships. I dreaded the day when I had to say goodbye to my friends, but I knew it would come, sooner or later. When there are no 'hellos' of substance there is no need for goodbyes.

Joyce Rupp reminds us: 'The blessedness in the ache within us is that when we grieve over the farewells, we both give ourselves and find ourselves. We become one with whoever and whatever has met us on our journey. We choose to invest ourselves deeply even though we know that the investment might cost us the price of goodbyes and letting go.'

When the 'goodbye' day finally came it was a painful relocation. In fact, it felt like a dislocation, and it was hampered by varying interpretations of Salvation Army policy regarding moves. The farewell system is ingrained in our culture but there is confusion surrounding the transfer of allegiance to the incoming officer and the role of ongoing relationships. We followed a couple with two small children into our new appointment, and I want them to be able to stay in touch with their friends in this community. We officers need to find ways to adjust our relationships with soldiers rather than discard them.

Paul writes of this committed love (1 Thessalonians 2:7, 8, 19 *TNIV*): 'Just as a nursing mother cares for her children, so we cared for you. Because we loved you so much we were delighted to share with you not only the gospel of God, but our lives as well ... For what is our hope, our joy, or the crown in which we will glory in the presence of our Lord Jesus when he comes? Is it not you? Indeed, you are our glory and joy.'

CROSS-GENERATIONAL RELATIONSHIPS

Relational growth is enriched through cross-generational relationships. Psychologist Brenda Hunter reminds the woman at midlife that Erik Erikson's task of midlife is generativity – guiding the next generation: 'Not only does psychology tell us to pass the torch, but Scripture mandates it ... so we have no excuse for closing our hearts to younger women. And though our lifestyles may have changed over the past 30 years, our emotional needs as women have remained the same. All of us need someone to guide, encourage, and love us. And for a young woman, that someone is an older woman rich in life experience and wisdom who can help her define and shape her life.'

Titus 2 speaks about the relationship between older and younger women. For the younger woman it is a rewarding experience to seek out involvement with older women. In my 20s, with an infant and a toddler in the house, the highlight of my week was time spent with a group of Salvationist women on Monday mornings for Bible study and prayer. I was by far the youngest in that group, but that didn't matter, as it was a fellowship where each woman was embraced for who she was, regardless of age or achievement. These women gently modelled a maturity in Christ that I longed to attain. In this group I found a release for the tension I was experiencing as a wife, mother and officer; encouragement for my early attempts at song-writing; and a safe place to nurture my faith.

MALE/FEMALE RELATIONSHIPS

Our focus so far has been on woman-to-woman friendships. Male/female relationships get more complicated, but are possible. We often hear people say, 'I've married my best friend' and a friendship between husband and wife is to be cherished. Working together as officers can challenge that friendship or enrich it.

Outside of marriage there are inherent dangers in friendships between men and women, particularly as the relationship can become sexualised. But that doesn't have to happen. Christ modelled holy relationships with women, particularly with Mary of Bethany and Mary Magdalene. As a teenager I listened to Mary's song 'I Don't Know How to Love Him' from *Jesus Christ Superstar* and heard the tension in her singing, but knew that, because of who Christ was, the implied sexual nature of the relationship by the writer of that song was not an accurate picture of their connection. Yet the extreme depth of Mary's devotion to Christ (the anointing, at the cross, at the tomb) indicates that she cared intensely about this man, but with a passion that did not have to become sexualised.

If we accept that male/female friendships are possible between two mature, godly people, appropriate hedges can be placed around the friendship to protect each person, because while we may be mature and godly, we are also open to temptation. Suggested hedges are:

- both spouses are aware of the relationship and are OK with it;
- the other spouse knows in advance where and when the friends are going to meet;
- the man and woman are aware of potential sexual tension, and discuss it openly if it begins to impact the friendship;
- they make an agreement to meet only in public places;
- each is accountable to another person about the relationship.

On entering this kind of friendship it is vital to know where you are most vulnerable. Do you feel neglected in your marriage? Are compliments from your husband few and far between? If so, the attention a male friend gives can be very flattering – and dangerous. Do not be ignorant of your susceptible soft spots.

When these hedges are in place, a male/female friendship can enrich our lives in many ways. My male friends can say things to me that my female friends wouldn't consider saying, or don't even see. These relationships broaden who I am and teach me ways of relating to my husband and to other men I meet in both the business and social arena. They also affirm me as a woman, and stretch me intellectually and spiritually. And in the receiving I am able to let them glimpse the love of God that speaks from a feminine heart.

MAKING IT HAPPEN

The bottom line of relationship building is this: it takes time, work, determination and courage. Someone must make the phone call, set the date, name the place to gather. Sometimes it seems one-sided – don't resent that, but discuss it with the other person. It may be time to back off from the intensity of the friendship, or the other person is simply under a lot of pressure at home or at work and needs you to take charge for a while. In healthy relationships there is an ebb and flow – one receives, the other gives – then the balance shifts again. Give the benefit of the doubt, but address it honestly. We are busy women and the urgent can so easily crowd out the essential. Give relationships the priority in your calendar they deserve.

Relationships don't just happen, they need to be worked at. Anything worth having in this life takes work. When I am with my friend I must be *with* her. I want to be willing to listen, to laugh, to weep, to ask the hard questions and to answer them as well. This kind of deep relationship involves giving and receiving potentially painful feedback.

As for courage, yes a caring, committed friendship does take courage. When I hear that my friend is going through a difficult time my first inclination is to rescue her, pull her out of the muddy puddle she is sitting in. The courage of the relationship allows me

168

simply to sit with her in the mud, be available to her in silence, in waiting, and, if she desires, in problem-solving or planning. It also includes risking being seen in my totality by another's eyes, with the courage to believe she will still love me when she has seen the ugliness of my motives and behaviour.

SPOKEN AGENDA

When spending an hour with my friend Janice she knew I was having a difficult time with some areas of my life. She simply asked me, 'How can I be a friend to you today? Do you want to talk about what is going on for you, or do you want to forget about it for a while and talk about other things?' At another time she asked: 'Will it be more helpful to talk about this just now, or would you like to pray about it together?'

It is OK to be intentional about how long we are able to stay and to say to each other, 'This is what we want to cover today.' I've found that to be very helpful, as often our time together is limited, and it is beneficial to leave each other's presence knowing we accomplished what was important to both of us.

ACCOUNTABILITY

Mutual accountability can also have a place in friendship, if that's something you need from each other. It can be set in a specific time frame or involve particular questions you will ask each other when you get together. While I don't have a formalised accountability partner I do have people in my life who are good at asking me hard questions and not letting me get away with easy answers. They know my heart, the dignity and the human weaknesses that exist within me, and are willing to confront the weaknesses and call forth the dignity.

SPIRITUAL CONVERSATION

We may not realise our hunger for spiritual conversation until we have been the recipient of it, and are able to appreciate how it has fed our soul. Eugene Peterson, best known for *The Message*, describes this spiritual counsel as 'easy, prayerful conversation between companions engaged in a common task'. He points out that Jesus used the word 'friends' to describe his disciples in John 15:15, therefore setting us in 'a non-hierarchical, open, informal, spontaneous company of Jesus-friends, who verbally develop relationships of responsibility and intimacy by means of conversation'. How I long for open, honest conversation about spiritual things, for conversation about how the Scripture I read today is affecting me, revealing God to me in a clearer way or puzzling me. I cannot have that kind of conversation with everyone I know, but how grateful I am for those God has placed in my life who are available for those words and questions! Sometimes I am the one who has to steer the conversation in a more spiritual direction but when I do we are both enriched.

IN OUR CONTROL

Smede's words provide a fitting conclusion on this topic: 'Each moment is a new beginning. In every decision we swipe the Fates aside and take charge of our future with another person. We change our mind, we improvise, we adjust, we suffer, we wait, we forgive, we move in and out of love and we accommodate ourselves to the shifting scenes of our life as we move from stage to stage on our journey. And we can make all our moves, freely, on the foundation we created by our commitments. We listen, we stay awake, we stay in tune with reality, we forgive, we stay honest [and] the final truth about us – the truth that matters most – is our power to keep our human relationships alive, our power to make and keep commitments. We cannot survive, cannot preserve our humanity, without enduring relationships of caring love.

NEW LOCATION

I almost forgot to mention play. I was with a friend recently, talking seriously for quite some time, when she said: 'Do you have time to play?' We drove off into the country and spent time browsing the picturesque little shops.

A few years ago I attended a women's conference. Afterwards, five of us went across the street to watch a baseball game. We had a blast. Our team lost but it didn't matter one bit. We were together, the sunset was glorious and life was good. Girlfriends are good for playing as well as for serious spiritual conversation. Chocolate definitely tastes better when shared!

So can you go for it? Can you work to deepen the friendships you already have? And will you courageously seek out new relationships? Perhaps you need to pick up the phone today and renew connections with a friend from your past. It truly is amazing how nourishing an afternoon with a well-loved friend can be. I hope that gift is yours soon.

Eleven

When the Darkness Comes

And so the sun went down and the woods got dark,
and with the darkness came the tears.
There I was, huddled in the rain, shivering,
and the only thing I could do was pray for the dawn.

Ken Gire

ONE day, the darkness falls. It may come early in officership, through the loss of a child or parent. In midlife years it may manifest itself as bouts of depression or the spiritual 'dark night of the soul' in the anguish of marital discord or the sorrow of wayward teens. Life-threatening illness, widowhood or consuming loneliness may be ours in later years of life. But whatever the time line, it can come suddenly – a tragedy that occurs with no prior warning – or it may stealthily creep up on us, so insidiously that we are caught unaware. At times we find ourselves able to welcome others into our darkness, as did Job with his three comforter friends. But there are other instances when we must battle the darkness alone, as did Jesus while his most trusted companions lay asleep in the garden.

Sometimes, its appearance is fleeting. Other times, it slinks in and out like a moody cat, dancing on the edges of our days, and we find ourselves greeting it with Simon and Garfunkel's words, 'Hello, darkness, my old friend' when it crawls up on our lap. For others it becomes a constant companion, one as central to our existence as that grimy, ragged security blanket our daughter dragged around until she was three. Whatever the character or time frame, the darkness we experience is real and powerful, and can smother our marriage, family life, ministry and spirit with its shroud of despair.

WOMEN FROM THE WORD

Biblical women were not immune to the darkness and despair this chapter is addressing. Again, just as we found in looking at motherhood, we do not have full portraits of women in many of these situations so are limited to what is actually recorded in the Bible, but we can use what we know about women and about ourselves to attempt to imagine and understand the depths of the darkness four biblical women faced.

RESIGNATION

Consider first the widow at Zarephath whom we encounter in 1 Kings 17:7-24. Due to a terrible drought she was making preparations for a final meal for herself and her son when Elijah approached her for some water and bread. What a cruel request! Doesn't he know she has nothing, that she is preparing her final meal before she would die? She was resigned to being without hope. To her way of thinking that was better than vainly believing life could get better. Yet as the story unfolds, in her obedient response to Elijah's request, the oil and flour are replenished each day and she does not starve to death. Her despair slowly turns to hope – until the day her son dies. Perhaps within her spirit she railed: 'Why didn't you just let us die together? Now I will be alone. Elijah, you and your God are playing me for a fool. How could you allow me to hope again?

DEATH

As a character from C. S. Lewis's *The Magician's Nephew* says: 'You know how it feels if you begin hoping for something that you want desperately badly – you almost fight against the hope because it is too good to be true; you've been disappointed so often before.'

A descriptive passage on the loss of a loved one is found in John 11, the account of Mary and Martha's grief over the death of their brother Lazarus. As expected from what we know of Mary and Martha from other passages, the sisters had different reactions to their grief. Martha was a woman who acted, and 'when Martha heard that Jesus was coming she went out to meet him' (verse 20). Judging by Jesus' response, her words to him were those of accusation: 'If you had been here, my brother would not have died.' Their subsequent conversation led to the words of Jesus which have brought faith and comfort to so many: 'I am the resurrection and the life. He who believes in me will live, even though he dies, and whoever lives and believes in me will never die.' He followed that tremendous statement with a challenge to Martha: 'Do you believe this?'

How different was Mary's reaction and Jesus' response to it! Mary had stayed in the home when Martha went to meet Jesus, and it wasn't until Martha returned, relaying Jesus' request to see Mary, that she left her place of mourning and went to him. Her first words to him were the same as her sister's: 'If you had been here, my brother would not have died' (verse 32) but it may be that in her case they were not words of accusation but simply an acknowledgement of his power. Jesus' response at first was non-verbal: 'When Jesus saw her weeping … he was deeply moved in spirit and troubled' – or as Barclay suggests, 'so that an involuntary groan burst from him, and he trembled with deep emotion'. When confronted with Mary's grief, we see Jesus' sorrow, expressed in his own subsequent weeping (verse 35).

DESPAIR

While grief was at the forefront of Martha and Mary's emotional response to the death of their brother, grief is joined by despair in the heartcry of Mary Magdalene at the tomb. She had watched the horror of the crucifixion unfold from a distance, then quietly watched as the body was placed in the tomb. Lutheran pastor and writer Walter Wangerin describes it for us through Mary's eyes:

'Stone cold. And the stone is closed … What do I do? I don't know what to do. Nothing. The Sabbath has started. So what? So, if I pray I'll be mouthing the sounds. Nothing. And if I pray a vain repetition, what then? Will Heaven be offended? *Well, Heaven has offended me!* Joseph's stone is like the period that stops the sentence. Boom! – the story's done. And when the story's over, the very air is empty. No place for me. No home for my soul. Silence. Why do I keep standing here? It's dark. It's midnight. Everyone's gone home. Except me. Abandoned. Nothing.'

Yet she returns. She came again at the dawning, drawn in this last grasping for the man who knew her and loved her and who had literally saved her life – and her soul. While her words are few at the tomb, the panic in her voice is palpable as she encountered the unknown man: 'They have taken away my Lord, and I don't know where they have put him.' Not only has the light been snuffed out, not only have the promises been voided, but now someone has played a cruel, cruel joke at her expense – even the body is gone.

During Holy Week meetings I have appeared in character as Mary Magdalene, and it is at this moment, before the turning, before the recognition of Jesus, that the cascade of emotion has drowned the Mary I am – sorrow, fear, rage, despair, all mixed together. And then there is the turning, the seeing, the dawning, and she knows it for what it is: 'Terror. Fear and wonder and love all mixed in me … it's a killing terror, isn't it? Exquisite and sharp – a painful, impossible joy.'

The drawback in using these stories to explore how women can face darkness is that all four women experience happy endings of the greatest kind – their loved one came back to life miraculously. But it is not the endings that are the focus of this chapter; it is the acceptance of the depth of emotion, the 'in the midst of it' pain, the 'cloud of unknowing' that we can't control. We are sometimes left hanging, believing in our depths that God is at work but walking zombie-like through the interminable days and holding on through the terror of the endless, sleepless nights until the dawn breaks through.

UNEXPECTED TRAGEDY

And so it comes to us, as to these women from the past. The settings may not look the same but the emotion is a collective one, constant through the centuries. The darkness falls upon us. It comes in the form of an untimely phone call from the emergency room, the malignant biopsy report, the startling death, the world turned upside down. We know the stories. We've heard them countless times through our days of ministry but now they don't belong to another, they are ours to own, the next chapter in our narrative. You were buttering toast or putting on your coat when the phone rang, and you will always remember that moment when the clock stood still for you. 'Come quickly,' the voice pleads, but you know deep within that you can do nothing to change the outcome.

WIDOWHOOD

It comes as a sudden blow or as a long, poignant farewell, as our husband is lost to this world, but finds a home in Heaven. As officers, not only do we lose a spouse but also the man who has partnered us in ministry. It is a double loss. As active officers we face the question of appointment. Can we maintain the responsibilities we had shared while coping with the grief or do we need to move to a different assignment, which may then add another level of stress to the time of loss? Will we have any input into that decision? If we are retired, we face the loss of the dreams we had shared for our retirement years, as well as the changes we may need to make in living arrangements. We are now the outsider, the widow in a culture of married people. It is no longer 'us' it is only 'me'.

Beyond these practical implications of widowhood, an intensity of darkness may descend upon a woman as she moves through the waves of grief. Poet Luci Shaw spoke of her loss of her husband in *God in the Dark*, pouring out her grief immediately after his death and in the days which stretched endlessly beyond it: 'I feel detached, amputated, flat, numb with tears that will not come. But it was pure relief to cry, at last to begin to feel and know the depth of my missing him, that I am a real person with real grief about real bereavement. I want those feelings of grief to have their way with me, so that I'll know I'm all there as the pain presses in. Death has sealed off those married years like a capped bottle of perfume. Our marriage cannot be lost or shattered. Nothing can touch it now. It's safe – one of my treasures laid up in Heaven where no moth-like resentment or rusty dissolution can erode it. Bereavement, death, is radical surgery on a marriage. Now the anesthesia is beginning to wear off. The nerves tingle, the pain reflexes twitch. I am beginning to feel the rawness of amputation.'

Luci gives us a glimpse of her personal loss and it is a road every widow must walk for herself, no matter how many people form part of her life.

MARITAL STRUGGLE

When the marriage is going well, the sharing of ministry is a source of joy in our lives. But when we are struggling within the marriage, particularly if in corps ministry, the need to work closely together can magnify and multiply the marital problems, leaving each spouse with no place to hide. Officer marriage can resemble Siamese twins at times. Imagine being a conjoined twin and not getting along with your sister! Twins who find themselves conjoined do not have the responsibility for the joining. It was, depending on your perspective, an act of God or a freak of nature. As married officers we're hooked together by forces outside ourselves but we have had a hand in the choosing, although we may try to blame God for his role in it.

When it goes bad, the options are limited. The counsellor may recommend a therapeutic separation but he or she doesn't understand how trapped you feel, and how that couldn't possibly work. You sit in the meeting on Sunday, listening to your husband preach and you feel that both he and you are frauds, encouraging others to love in a way that you yourselves (or one of you, at least) find impossible. Either the marriage or the ministry has to give, but neither does, and you end up being the one who is broken. You can ask for an appointment that would change the dynamics by giving more space to each of you, with the goal of putting the pieces back together in the marriage, but that may not be possible, or may cause more discomfort. Strategies for repair of the relationship may help, but don't change the intensity of the pain or the feeling of failure over our inability to make it work.

Realise, through the darkness, that you are not alone. The system sets up a scenario that generally does not aid fragile marriage. It may be necessary to step aside from the ministry for a time to protect the marriage.

LONELINESS

Novelist May Sarton writes of women who are alone: 'Loneliness is the poverty of self; solitude is the richness of self.' As active officers we're surrounded by people every day who move in and out of our lives yet there still can be a profound loneliness. It is, as we noted in chapter 10, the absence of connection, and is as much a function of our own emotional isolation as it is of our circumstances. We can be alone yet not lonely, but it is in our poverty of attitude and choice that loneliness has its power.

DEPRESSION

Depression is a term, a diagnosis, our culture has overused. But when it has you in its talons, it has you. At its worst, it is a swallowing up that seemingly has no floor to its pit. As the senses are dulled, the world becomes entirely washed in shades of grey, posted with a warning, 'No colours allowed to enter here.'

Two descriptions may help: 'a form of "brain pain" that is practically unendurable. Not only is the face of God eclipsed, but their own souls are in eclipse' (Dunlop), and 'dry, weary, patient pain' (Quinn). Musician Louis Armstrong's comment on the blues also fits: 'If you have to ask, you'll never know.'

However it manifests itself, depression is a serious illness diagnosed by the symptoms of unhappy mood, negative thought, low energy behaviour, various physical symptoms and anxiety. It is a dangerous, potentially deadly, condition and must be acknowledged and treated appropriately. As Christian psychologist Diane Langberg assures us: 'This disorder is not necessarily caused by difficulties with living, spiritual problems or lack of faith. Severe, biological depressions can happen through no fault of one's own, and need to be treated like any other medical illness.'

DARK NIGHT OF THE SOUL

A second cousin to depression is the spiritual place known historically as 'the dark night of the soul'. Generally experienced by those who have had a long, vibrant walk with Christ, it can come unexpectedly and settle upon us as a pall. Susan Muto describes it: 'We cannot see the dawn of a new day in the Lord unless we pass through a night when we must cope with our fears of darkness, our evil imaginings of pending doom, the inner tugs of war between that of us willing to take any risk to meet God and that of us wanting only a safe haven.'

Benedict Groeshel wrote of the illustration of an older man: 'His only consolation, he said, was in knowing he shared the terror and loneliness of Mary and Joseph when they hurried back to Jerusalem to search for the Christ Child who had been entrusted to them and lost through their own apparent negligence.' In this dark night God appears to be absent, and our usual means of worship and prayer are arid.

DOUBT

While doubt can be a factor in the dark night of the soul, doubt in its various forms can exist apart from the dark-night experience. Doubt is not often addressed within the Army, and when it is it is usually in the context of sin. Jackie Hudson is aware of the problem of doubt within Church circles: 'Christians who are struggling with doubt don't talk about it. They are ashamed of it. Or they have resigned themselves to living with it like they would an annoying headache.' As a minister of the gospel, what do you do with your doubts? Certainly you can't talk about them in your small group Bible study, especially if you're the teacher. There are sermons to prepare and preach, dying people to visit, and yet the demons of doubt churn away, causing you to be wary of your own judgment and words.

EVIL

We should not rule out the possibility that the darkness may be rooted in evil. While I do not think in the same kind of terms or images as someone like novelist Frank Perretti (*This Present Darkness, Piercing the Darkness*), I am familiar enough with evil to know that it exists, and that there is an evil force with power in this world. I don't like giving this force credit for power it doesn't have, nor do I like blaming it for my own foolishness, as in 'the devil made me do it', but the role of evil must be considered in situations where there is ongoing darkness that cannot be explained in other ways.

WHAT TO DO?

What can we do when the darkness comes? I wish it were as easy as a 1-2-3 list of steps to take, so that, as for Annie in the musical, you will know that 'the sun will come out tomorrow'. Yes, the sun will rise tomorrow, but you may be unable to see it or feel it, as the darkness within takes on a life of its own. You may be overwhelmed with how capricious the waves of grief are, how volatile the anger you feel (so unlike your usual self), or how much you want to follow Job's example and 'have it out with God'. Yet in the midst of all that is seething within us there are some things we can do to face the darkness with honesty and courage.

AVOID DENIAL

It is a truth that a wound causes trauma, a cut finger bleeds. While external bleeding can be staunched with a bandage, stitches or tourniquet, bleeding that is unseen is more dangerous. If ignored, internal bleeding can lead to death. If ignored, internal despair can lead to death. We can only repress emotional distress for a time;

after that, it erupts in physical expressions (high blood pressure, ulcers), behavioural reactions (out-of-control anger, lethargy) or spiritual disturbance (bitterness, disbelief). We don't need to be ashamed of our humanness. If we resort to a self-sufficient 'I can do it by myself role' we deny God's power to touch us where we most need him, and we portray a Christianity that can function quite well, thank you very much, without a Saviour. So we must see the darkness for what it is, not sugar coat it with platitudes or a shallow interpretation of the promises of Scripture. All things, we are told, will work together for good (given the conditions of Romans 8:28), but not all things are in themselves 'good'.

Susan Howatch writes often of this intermingling in her novels, as is illustrated by her words in *Absolute Truths*: 'The correct translation of that passage is actually: "All things intermingle for good to them that love God" ... It gives a better impression of synergy – the process where two different things are put together and make something quite new. If you just say: "All things work together for good" – as if the good and the bad are all stirred together like the ingredients of a cake which later emerges from the oven smelling wonderful – then the man who's dying of cancer will want to punch you on the jaw because he knows ... you're understating his pain and playing fast and loose with the reality of his suffering by implying that his disease is in the end a good thing. But if you say: "All things intermingle for good" you're implying that the good and the bad remain quite distinct ... The bad really is terrible and the good may seem powerless against that terrible reality, but when the good and the bad intermingle – not merge, but intermingle ...". "They form a pattern," said Jon, "as I pointed out a moment ago. The darkness doesn't become less dark, but that pattern which the light makes upon it contains the meaning which makes the darkness endurable."'

ENTERING THE DARKNESS
Henri Nouwen knows that the darkness needn't be avoided: 'People who have come to know the joy of God do not deny the

darkness, but they choose not to live in it. They claim that the light that shines in the darkness can be trusted more than the darkness itself, and that a little bit of light can dispel a lot of darkness. They point each other to flashes of light here and there and remind each other that they reveal the hidden but real presence of God.'

A classic work on the dark night of the soul is *The Cloud of Unknowing*. It tells us: 'You will seem to know nothing and to feel nothing except a naked intent toward God in the depths of your being. Try as you might, this darkness and this cloud will remain between you and your God ... but learn to be at home in the darkness. Return to it as often as you can, letting your spirit cry out to him whom you love.'

What does it mean to 'enter the darkness'? It means willingness to face the seething emotions within rather than running to our favourite distractions. It involves stepping aside from the intensity of the work to ask the questions nagging at our souls. It means praying Psalm 88, sitting under Elijah's broom tree or walking willingly into our private Gethsemane.

DON'T DEMAND ANSWERS

Our society is obsessed with a need to know. With the advent of the internet the new information superhighway has made it possible to know virtually everything, to find the answer to just about any question. When my son comes home with science homework involving some pretty obscure questions, most of the time we can find the answer. Just ask a search engine! The dilemma of the spiritual life is that we cannot know all the answers; in fact, when we demand to know, we shake our fist in God's face. Somehow, we have to come to a place of trust that doesn't demand to know, like novelist Annie Lamott's character, who 'tried to just accept things; to try not to figure out God's last name'.

In *Wishful Thinking*, Buechner writes: 'Maybe the reason God doesn't explain to Job why terrible things happen is that he knows what Job needs isn't an explanation. Understanding in terms of the divine economy why his children had to die, Job would still have to face their empty chairs at breakfast every morning. God doesn't reveal his grand design. He reveals himself. He doesn't show why things are as they are. He shows his face. And Job says, "I had heard of thee by the hearing of the ears, but now my eyes see thee." Even covered with sores and ashes, he looks oddly like a man who has asked for a crust and been given the whole loaf.'

In *If I Really Believe, Why Do I Have These Doubts?* Lynn Anderson sees it in a different light: 'There is nothing wrong with trying to understand our faith. But many of us try too hard. We attempt to explain the unexplainable, find out the undefinable, ponder over the imponderable, and unscrew the inscrutable ... Full faith gets down to the part of us that we cannot explain or quantify but that shapes the direction of our lives. God not only reveals his endless love and awesome holiness, but also veils his majesty in mystery and paradox that transcend comprehension. Full faith awakens all of our worlds and dances through them, touching us on multiple levels and moving us with profound force.'

WAITING

Hear the yearning in Sharon Hersh's words: 'I am learning that maturity is not the absence of longing, but it is the ability to wait in the loneliness. Waiting keeps me from hurrying into the next moment, so I don't have to stay in this one. Waiting invites me to change even if those I love do not. Waiting cultivates aching hope.'

How do you live with an aching hope? It raises another question: is it better to ache or to be numb to the longings? In our culture of instant gratification, having to wait for even a 'fast food' hamburger can be a chore, but to wait in a period of darkness with no promise that it will end in a specific time frame can be excruciating. However, that is where we most profoundly meet our God.

Henri Nouwen is so helpful on this subject: 'True patience is the opposite of a passive waiting in which we let things happen and allow others to make the decisions. Patience means to enter actively into the thick of life and to fully bear the suffering within and around us.'

FIGHTING INERTIA

In stark contrast to waiting in the unknown is the need to battle the darkness. While there may be times we need to sit and wait in the darkness, we cannot build upon darkness, and we must find ways to move from it. We must use care to make our 'cave' as uncomfortable as possible, for if we furnish it (in our mind or spirit) with comfortable lounge chairs and a warm afghan, then we run the danger of being too comfortable there, getting used to it and wanting to stay forever, and we will not be able to access the energy we need to move out of it.

In facing the desire for inertia, the wooing voice drones on and on: 'Don't think, don't feel, be numb.' We must find tangible ways to break the paralysing force that threatens to overcome us. Simple, everyday things can help, particularly if you're living alone. Make the effort to talk with someone every day, by phone or preferably in person, even if you have to be the one to initiate the conversation. Don't stand mute at the checkout counter at the supermarket. Speak. Find an opportunity to listen to someone for at least five minutes each day. If you are able, get up and walk – down the hall, through the neighbourhood, on the beach. Write. Now may be the time to begin to write a journal each day, even when the sight of a blank page seems daunting. Write of everyday things, write of your churning emotions, pour out your doubts and fears, both known and unknown. Write a letter, write a poem, let your bottled-up feelings escape through your pen.

Music deserves its own paragraph. As Andrew Greeley, novelist, sociologist and priest, says: 'What the world would be like without music? We would still be humans and life would go on but it would be much more difficult to mourn our losses and celebrate our loves.' So we turn to music in our mourning, in our losses, in our darkest times. The old hymns, which speak the scriptural truths in ways we can cling to, become our dearest friends in the darkness.

The songs in the night provide an aura of peace to us in the midst of our internal turmoil. The haunting melodies of the spirituals sing from an anguish that we can touch with our own heart's cry. Try the classics: Mahler and Tchaikovsky for the dark moods, Bach and Beethoven for 'the light of day', the rising passions of Gorecki's *Third Symphony*.

It may be that the words of a simple chorus will become the lifeline you need. A friend told me of her experience with a chorus I had written, 'God Cares for You'. We sang it at home league camp a number of years ago, and she had taken it as her prayer at that time, not knowing how much she would later need the promise of that song as she lay alone in a hospital bed, recovering from cancer surgery. She told me: 'It was as if I couldn't get away from those words: "God cares for you, you are precious in his sight; God cares for you, even through the darkest night." It was, for me, the darkest night I had ever experienced, but those four words gave me courage that the morning would come, and that I was his child.'

Listen, play, sing – even try your hand at composition – but let the notes seep into the deepest recesses of your soul. If your interests run in a different direction, art, film, poetry or fiction can speak to you during these days as well.

And in the darkness we can return to the old wells, as the chorus reminds us, where the waters are deep. Return to the times, the places, the friend, the spirit where you have been assured of God's presence. Relive those days, return to the disciplines that had brought you to them before, or to the disciplines that have kindled the fire within the saints of God through the centuries. Go where faith is nourished, so that your starving soul can be fed.

CLING TO WHAT YOU KNOW

Joyce Rupp reminds us of two great assurances: 'Do not fear' and 'I am with you'. She writes: 'I find great comfort in these assurances and clutch them to my empty heart when times are tough.' It is during times of darkness that we must reach deep into our pockets to pull out what we know to be true. I discovered Larry

Crabb's writing at the front end of a time of spiritual upheaval in my life. Reading *Inside Out* became a watershed experience for me, as the ideas he presented were very disrupting and very convicting. However, it was with a sense of relief that I read these words at the end of the book: 'Don't let the confusing parts of life rob you of confidence in the central truths of Christianity. Cling to what you know is true. There is a God, he loves you, he sent his son to die for your sins, he's promised to never leave you, and one day he'll return to make everything right ... ponder the importance of these unchanging truths until they become burning realities in your soul.'

As we cling to what we know, we will find in time that it is as Shaw describes: 'Just as the relationship in a marriage ebbs and flows, yet holds firm because of prior commitment, even when there is disagreement and love seems to have left, so too, because of prior commitment, we are held in continual relationship with God whether or not our level of faith is high, whether or not we feel that he is with us.'

Now may not the time to search out new ideas, but rather to hold on for dear life (and dear is what it is) until the darkness begins to lift.

FACING THE FEAR

Fear is a powerful emotion that feeds upon darkness. Experience tells us the anticipation is often worse than the dreaded experience: a visit to the dentist, an uncomfortable medical test or a long-postponed discussion of a sensitive issue.

My husband laughs fondly about the time he took an inner-city group of boys out in the woods for a camping trip. These kids who were so macho and so brave in the streetlights of their rough-and-tumble Philadelphia neighbourhood were petrified in the pitch black of the moonless night, miles from any electricity. Bringing our fears into the light allows us to face the fear head-on, and, in doing so, it is stripped of much of its power. Unfounded fear can be exposed for its deception, and realistic fear can be honestly evaluated and addressed. When framed in the context of 'What's the worst that can happen?' any improvement on 'the worst' can be bearable.

IN COMMUNITY
Writing in *The Cry of the Soul*, Dan Allender and Tremper Longman recognise the importance of the presence of other people in our lives in times of anguish: 'I must sorrow, even despair, in communion with others who live with some awareness of the same cry of dereliction and the same hope of resurrection.' A friend hosts a nightly radio phone-in show and he concludes each broadcast with these words: 'When the going gets tough, don't give up, don't give in, remember, you don't have to journey alone.' It is counsel that is especially appropriate for the dark times. We don't have to journey alone. We have the power of the Spirit of God who has promised to be with us, and we have the privilege of being part of a community of believers, and of a Movement that is at its best when tragedy strikes, particularly when it shifts into crisis mode.

In specific ways, help from a variety of sources is available. A medical examination to rule out physical problems, along with discussion of medication if the depression is clinical in nature, can give you the ability to do the needed soulwork. While some may be hesitant to start medication, it can help to stabilise an individual so they can begin to work on the issues that contributed to the depression. As Bringle teaches, it is necessary for the totality of the human person to be physically healthy in order to be able to undertake the difficult demands of soul-making: 'Far from offering an escape from these demands, medication can facilitate a fuller engagement with them.'

Perhaps it is time to work with a counsellor. It's easy to know what we would say to someone else in our situation, but in the midst of it we cannot see clearly, and being accompanied by a wise guide on this leg of the journey can be invaluable. Effective biblical counselling can strengthen you in ways that may surprise you, and it may be the way God desires to work in your life to shed light on what is sinful within you, and what needs to be affirmed in you as well. It may be disrupting to the patterns developed over the years just to survive, but it provides freedom from bondage to those patterns, and courage to move forward. When stuck in a dark time, what we try to do often doesn't have any effect. Remember, insanity is defined as doing the same thing over and over, expecting different results. It's time to learn new ways of thinking and behaving, so you can move toward the light of healing and hope.

Another option, especially if the darkness is considered to be primarily spiritual in nature, is to seek the assistance of a spiritual director. Rather foreign to many Salvation Army officers, this concept has been used historically in the Roman Catholic Church, but now is experiencing an upsurge in at least some evangelical camps. Spiritual direction can provide us with accountability and insight in the matters of our faith, while drawing our eyes inward, upward and outward.

Don't be afraid to ask for what you need, or admit you don't know what you need.

KEEP ON

Let's return to Walter Wangarin and his instructions to Mary Magdalene: 'Mary, do this: even in your despair, observe the rituals. It is the Sabbath; then let it be the Sabbath after all. Pray your prayers. However hollow and unsatisfying they may feel, God can fill them. God is God, who made the world from nothing – and God as God can still astonish you. He can make of your mouthings a prayer – and of your groanings a hymn. Observe the ritual. Prepare your spices. Return on Sunday, even to this scene of your sorrow, expecting nothing but a corpse, planning nothing but to sigh once more and to pay respects. One story is done indeed, my Magdalene. You're right. You've entered the dark night of the soul. But another story – one you cannot conceive of (it's God who conceives it!) – starts at sunrise. And the empty time between, while sadly you prepare the spices, is in fact preparing you! ... Come again on Sunday, Mary, and see how it is that God makes saints.'

And so we, like Mary, pull ourselves out of bed, pray our prayers and go through the motions of living for one more day. We allow God to do his work in us as we 'prepare our spices', until the day comes when we once again are startled by the bird singing outside our window, or we realise that the tones of the sunset are once again in colour rather than black and white.

FOR A PURPOSE

Buechner prays the following prayer: '"Almighty God, are you true?" When you are standing up to your neck in darkness, how do you say yes to that question? You say yes with your fingers crossed. You say yes with your heart in your mouth. It is still a dark world but the darkness is different because he keeps getting born into it.'

We do have the hope of a believer, that God is in the midst of what we are going through and that he is walking through it with us, actively using what is happening to us and in us to stretch us and to draw us closer to his heart. Michael Mounds puts it like this: 'In all your journey as a believer, you will have two categories of spiritual experiences. One is tender, delightful and loving. The other can be quite obscure, dry, dark and desolate. God gives us the first one to gain us; he gives us the second to purify us.' Ultimately, the image found in the promise of Isaiah 45:3 holds: 'I will give you the treasures of darkness, riches stored in secret places, so that you may know that I am the Lord, the God of Israel, who summons you by name.'

Twelve

Towards the End of the Path

The Road goes ever on and on
Down from the door where it began,
Now far ahead the Road has gone,
And I must follow, if I can,
Pursuing it with eager feet
Until it joins some larger way.

J. R. R. Tolkien

DEVELOPMENTAL psychologist Erik Erikson speaks of old age as offering the psychosocial crisis of integrity versus despair: 'Will I be able to maintain integrity with the foundation I've built my life upon, or will I no longer be able to live by that? Will I be able to live from a place of wisdom, or will I settle for dogmatism, for being so stuck in where I've been that there's no room for new light?'

A visit to the neighbourhood nursing home affirms Erikson's theory and suggests that despair is winning the battle over joy for some, particularly elderly, people. As Salvation Army women, having spent 20, 30 or 40 years in active ministry, we are not exempt from Erikson's crisis, and must carefully consider the implications for our work and our rest. What happens when it is time to retire?

I've got to admit, I look forward to that day. Beyond the obvious benefit of being able to experience Christmas as a normal person, I look forward to following the various threads of interests and gifting that are only peripheral right now due to the requirements

191

of my appointment. For some, retirement goals may be to choose where you are going to live, to experience the fun of furnishing a home of your own or the freedom to wear green or red instead of navy blue. The relief from the stress of officership, with its resulting decrease in blood pressure, is one of the biggest pluses I hear retired officers speak of, although a sense of loss due to the enmeshment of officership and identity may be experienced by some.

Like each of the other seasons, this final one brings positive and negative aspects. While we do want to 'accentuate the positive' it's not always possible to 'eliminate the negative' from our lives, and in our older years, attempting to do so may lead to denial instead of healthy living. Instead we can face them honestly and courageously, changing those we can and accepting those we cannot.

WOMEN FROM THE WORD
At age 52 I can look at 'older' women with a combination of curiosity and respect (but realising the distance isn't as wide as it used to be!). What makes the difference, I wonder, between those who thrive on the opportunities of retirement and those who self-destruct? We can bring that curiosity and respect to incidents recorded within the Scriptures involving older women. For our purpose of looking at old age, we will assume that 'widow' implies age, although that may not necessarily be true.

THE ABILITY TO LAUGH
Sarah was an old woman who laughed. Actually, she got in trouble with God because she laughed, even though she had good reason to do so. After all, she was told she would have a baby at 90! As she said in Genesis 18:12: 'After I am worn out and my master is old, will I now have this pleasure?' Even though she lied about having laughed (she was afraid), she ended up naming Isaac 'he laughs', remarking after his birth, 'God has brought me laughter, and everyone who hears about this will laugh at me' (Genesis

21:6). Sarah's spontaneous reaction of laughter tells us she was able to laugh at herself and at her circumstances. She was a woman who could experience joy. She reminds us that no matter our age, we can continue to laugh. We don't need to sink into despondency and stay there.

THE ABILITY TO GIVE
In Luke 21:2 we can look through the eyes of Jesus at a woman no one else noticed, a poor widow placing her meagre offering in the Temple's treasury. In comparison to the rich contributors, her gift was minuscule, but in the eyes of the Christ, her gift was symbolic of her generosity of spirit. A woman in the waning years of life can choose to live lavishly, with a largesse of spirit that goes far beyond the balance in her bank account, and gives simply out of the joy of giving.

THE ABILITY TO PRAY
We get another glimpse of a widow through Jesus' eyes in the story of the persistent widow in Luke 18. She was a woman with the continued ability to persevere, or, as Jesus explained, 'to cry out to him [God] day and night' (Luke 18:7). She was only a woman, with no man to protect or take care of her, and in Jesus' story she could be seen in a negative light as a nagging woman, but Jesus praised her ability to persist until she received what she needed.

THE ABILITY TO HAVE IMPACT
Turning again to the Old Testament we encounter a fascinating figure in the wise woman from Tekoa who came to David (2 Samuel 14). In desiring to help David be reconciled with Absalom, Joab was unsure of his ability to reach David so devised a plan that involved a woman who would come to David with a story of two sons. Was she a pawn, or was she actually an effective actress who played a role in God's great drama in the life of David? She was a woman who took quite a risk and made a lasting impact on the life of David and the history of the people of Israel.

THE ABILITY TO HOPE

Our last snapshot of an older woman in the Scriptures is Anna in the Temple, whose story begins in Luke 2:36. At the point of Jesus' presentation in the Temple she is at least 84 years old, and perhaps as old as 100. She 'never left the Temple but worshipped night and day, fasting and praying' (Luke 2:37). Here is a woman of hope. She was waiting for the child promised for the redemption of Jerusalem, and her hope was fulfilled that day. God may not have called us to spend years and years in the temple, but he does call us to model Anna's aura of hope.

DIFFICULTIES IN THE TRANSITION

One day you're in the midst of a vibrant ministry, the next day you're a retired officer. You desire to be a generous woman who prays, who lives in the spirit of joy and hope and who continues to have impact upon her world, but things have changed. You've lost the status your active officership and appointment gave you. You may have moved to your dream home in your dream community but don't know anyone in that town. You've got to decide how active to become in the local corps or church, and where your retirement 'niche' is going to be. You may be experiencing health difficulties. And if you are married, your husband is experiencing the same things, which may be affecting him in different ways.

LOSS OF MINISTRY

For some, the difficult part of retirement is the feeling of being put out to pasture, cut off from a beloved ministry. For those in pastoral ministry, the loss of a congregation is difficult, as well as the loss of a structured life, with specific duties to be performed each day. A friend approaching retirement told me, 'I know I want to minister to women, but I don't know how that's going to happen, especially if I don't have a base to operate from.' After 30 or 40 years in a highly structured, heavily scheduled daily ministry, the next day we wake up and everything has changed.

LOSS OF IDENTITY

Women officers face not only the loss of a ministry but also a loss of identity. Issues of enmeshment surround marriage and family but also affect self, especially if not dealt with well throughout the ministry. For those who served in leadership positions, the fall may be fast and furious. One day you are Commissioner Jones, and the next day you are Jane Jones, retired, waiting in the doctor's surgery to get your blood pressure checked, or slipping into the local women's ministry meeting as just one of the members. It may be a strange but welcome change, but it's not always an easy adjustment. Suddenly you are out of the information loop. Nobody is asking for your input, and someone else is sitting in *your* chair in the office or filling *your* pulpit. No one is sitting in front of you, pouring out their hearts over a broken marriage or their fear for their children. You no longer have the status or standing that being 'the officer' provided. While these issues may affect your husband more than you, there still may be identity problems that women have to face.

PHYSICAL DECLINE

You may move into retirement healthy and active, or you may begin to suffer from physical problems that will limit your new ventures. As with any period of life, good nutrition, exercise and appropriate sleep will help, but physical limitations may simply have to be accepted. We've had practice with this before, accommodating the changes that puberty, pregnancy, lactation and menopause bring to our bodies, even finding ways to laugh about them – and to make the needed adjustments to function effectively.

ISOLATION

For some, isolation and loneliness become demons to be encountered for the first time in retirement. The first few weeks of relative solitude may be welcome after the clamour of active officership, but it's necessary to find balance, and not become a recluse. We watched this happen to my mother-in-law after her husband died. From my perspective, her home went from being her castle to a prison, and for at least 12 years she left her home only if someone else made the arrangements and strongly encouraged her to do so. She appeared content to do this, but I knew she still had much to offer others. She could have visited in the nursing home across the street, participated in the corps life or opened her home to others, as she had so often earlier in life. We need to be reminded that who we are doesn't change with the word 'retired'. We can choose to live an integrated, relational life well into our later years if we recognise the dangers of stagnation and continue to extend who we are to others.

AS THE ARMY CHANGES

As I write these words I am particularly aware of the changes that have occurred within the Army in the 30 years since I was a cadet. The surface ones are obvious: for the first few years of my officership I strapped myself into my high-collar uniform and bonnet, and felt like Scarlet O'Hara being laced into a corset, coming to associate Sundays with physical discomfort rather than freedom of worship. Technological innovations, especially the introduction of the computer, have made some aspects of the work easier, although for some the computer may seem more enemy than friend. My son Andrew began piano lessons for the first time aged 18, and it's obvious that learning a new skill as an adult is more difficult than at the age of nine. Other changes, such as the increase in staff, fewer meetings and the introduction of praise and worship music make the Army look different from the way it was 40, or even 20, years ago.

There have also been changes on a more ideological level. For some, these have brought sadness and fear that the Army may no longer be what it was called to be. As the Army moves to be relevant in contemporary times it faces the danger of leaving behind the previous generation. It's a dilemma, as Niebuhr reminds us, because: 'It is no easy task to build up the faith of one generation and not destroy the supports of the religion of the other.' Even at 52

I feel some of the same angst, particularly when it appears at times that the baby is being thrown out with the bathwater.

Officership itself is changing as well – too fast for some, not fast enough for others. The outward identification that defined holiness in the first half of the 20th century has changed drastically. Are we still a holiness movement as it used to be defined? What are the non-negotiables that make the Army 'the Army'? What does the retired officer do as he or she looks on, powerless to stem the tide that seems to be washing over the Movement?

During an officers' retreat I was reminded of the role older Salvationists have in passing on the torch. For people new to the Army, 'good old Army' songs are foreign and some of the practices make little sense unless you are aware of the huge effect the Army had in past years on the lives of many people – families immersed in poverty and alcoholism, children raised in homes without running water. It is essential to tell the stories and sing the songs, explaining how God used this motley band of believers to bring the presence of Christ to so many – and the continuing stories of how Christ still moves.

REGRETS

Eunice Vanderlaan relates from her own experience: 'I entered congregational ministry unwilling but found it worthwhile, exciting work. I went in crying and I came out crying. We had noticed earlier that there seemed to be two types of pastors who entered retirement. There were those who bore their battle scars but who nonetheless had embraced the ministry and taken their children with them through the heavy weather. They had sunk deep roots in their congregations and had drawn from the nourishment that was there. Then there were those who emotionally had held back, so their families held back, as a way of protecting themselves from ever being hurt. We noticed that when they reached retirement age, they had this numb look and manner about them. Recognising the potential for pain, but unwilling to miss the nourishing joy, we decided to put our roots down deep among the people.'

Eunice made a deliberate choice early on in ministry to put down deep roots and aimed to avoid that 'numb look and manner' she had seen in other retired ministry leaders. Hers is only one area in which regrets can surface. On entering retirement it may be that you have regrets about the priorities you set, especially with regards to your children. They may have moved far away, your relationship may be strained or they may accuse you of choosing the Army above their interests. You may regret the lack of impact you made as an officer, feeling your work really didn't do much to change lives like you thought it would in your early days of idealism. Maybe you spent too much time working and not enough time being a child of God. Regrets come in a variety of sizes and shapes, but ultimately they must be faced with honesty, repentance and restitution if needed, and then given over to the graciousness of God. Continuing to live in a state of regret allows the root of bitterness to take hold and colour the remainder of your days.

LEAVING A LEGACY

While it is likely that reflecting on the end of a working life may raise some regrets it is also an opportunity to consider the legacy that has been/is being left for those who come behind. On her retirement, Eva Burrows, the 13th General of The Salvation Army, reflected on her officership: 'I would like to feel that The Salvation Army is known more as a church and not just a social service agency. I would not mind so much if I'm forgotten, as long as the Army has grown. I hope I will be remembered as a General for the people, and especially a General for youth, because I believe in giving youth their place. They challenge us, shake us up and help us to move forward. There are many things I hope for, but if you ask me my ambition I would say, very simply and humbly, my ambition is just to please God.'

Certainly, any officer could find agreement with her final statement. It may be that your legacy is found in the sentiment of Proverbs 31:28: 'Her children arise and call her blessed', or as Mary prayed in the Magnificat: 'From now on all generations will call me blessed, for the Mighty One has done great things for me – holy is his name.' Perhaps your legacy will simply be that you were kind to those with little experience of kindness in their lives, or that you took someone under your wing and showed them what it was like to live like Jesus.

OPPORTUNITIES IN THE TRANSITION

We joke with friends that when they retire the husband is going to get a job at the local supermarket, but given the absence of health concerns, there is a window of a few years when a retired officer can explore options for employment that have only been a dream over the years of active ministry. In considering the kind of skills developed as an officer there are hundreds of jobs the retired officer could perform. As well, there may be temporary assignments he or she can fill within the Army – where there has been a breakdown of some kind, or in a short-term assignment to complete a specific task. A friend is working in post-retirement service in such a way, but made sure that she asked for – and got – a 'grandmother's clause' so that she has some flexibility in pursuing the family interests that are so important to her.

EXPLORING OF IDENTITY

While other seasons of life are better known for asking the question, 'Who am I?' that is a question which can be revisited in retirement. What is the core of my identity? Who have I become? Who do I want to be known as? Since the pressure of time and responsibilities have lessened or been removed, the early retirement years can explore new options and focus on developing character traits and gifts that have been buried during the years of 'active' ministry. We had a night when we invited our corps members to share their gifts with each other, singing, speaking, bringing cookies. Mary, aged 78, came dressed in purple, and I loved the freedom expressed in the Jenny Joseph poem she recited, 'Warning', found in the anthology *When I Am an Old Woman I Shall Wear Purple*. It was a vivid reminder that as we grow older we can be freed from the harness of expectations. Life is not over at 65, as we have the ability to continue to grow and stretch until the day we die. Perhaps it is best expressed by the comment made by a 90-year-old woman upon being urged to slow down: 'Slow down? Heavens, no! I want to die with my diary full!'

CHOICE

Yes, for the first time in many years we have unlimited choices. For some it is an exciting time – choosing where to live, what to wear and how to spend your time. But for others the lack of structure is a difficult transition to make. You wake up in the morning and if you want to you can stay in bed until noon. Or you can get up, exercise and meet someone for coffee. If your daughter calls and asks you to come for a few days, you can do it without taking vacation or getting others to cover your responsibilities. The trick is not to get overwhelmed with the magnitude of choices but to relax into the options before you.

REHEARSAL THEOLOGY

Killinger suggests: 'Retirement is a great time to learn about rehearsal theology, if one has never understood it before. It is a time for retrospection, for looking back across the hills and valleys of one's own existence and noting where the Almighty God has intervened in one's path, lifting a burden here and introducing a surprise there! We need to trace our journey – write our autobiography, as it were – and realise how wonderful the God of the covenant has been.'

What a life-giving concept! It is a time to tell your story, to yourself and to others. I love to hear how God was preparing the way, of how he came through for his daughters. Don't wait for someone else to do it at your funeral. Do it now, in bits and pieces or as a narrative recorded for others to hear.

In our appointment at Canton Corps, Ohio, there were many Titus 2 women, and I would encourage our younger women to listen to the stories, to go and talk with Ann, Joyce, Virginia, Jean,

Judy, Maxine, Inez, Joann, Verda, Lil and many others – because they were so rich in experience and so willing to share from those riches.

In a fascinating book entitled *Storying Ourselves: a Narrative Perspective on Christians in Psychology,* a number of prominent psychologists wrote their personal stories for the anthology. Listen to the voices of three women on the process. Mary Vander Goot asked: 'How can I tell the story of my life? It is not a single strand that I can trace from the beginning to now. Rather it is a complex mingling of things that rearrange as time changes me, and the complete story is not yet clear.'

Vivian Nix-Early wrote: 'I took up the invitation to write this chapter as but another opportunity for outreach; to witness to what the Lord will do with a life for no other reason than love. Recounting the story has confirmed my parentage and my role in the family of God. It has made me know even more that I am God's child.'

Hendrika Vande Kemp asked and answered the harder questions: 'Why should I tell my story? It isn't the story of every woman, only of one individual, one of God's unique creatures. Do I have a right to tell my story? Will my story lead people to dismiss me even further, render me more invisible? Or will the telling render me, finally, irreversibly real? Thus, it is not at all merely my story, but my witness to the gospel, testimony that God recognises us in all our uniqueness, that for each of us there is the story that climaxes in the hope of resurrection.'

LAUGHTER

As you tell the stories, be sure to include the funny ones as well. Sarah got into trouble with her laughter because she doubted God, not because she laughed. A spirit of joy and laughter is contagious. As old age progresses it is easy to buy into the 'woe is me' litany of aches and pains – and they are real. In no way do I want to minimise the pain and struggle of old age, but the ability to smile and to laugh is a life-giving contribution to others and self.

GIVING

Like the widow in Luke 21:2, a woman in retirement can continue to give, whether from her riches or from her poverty. For some officers, retirement is a time with more flexibility in spending – and giving – than they have ever had. Others may have fewer assets but continue to have the ability to give from who they are. I have watched as women have slipped a struggling young officer a little money, as meals have been prepared for them, as babysitting has been offered and a meaningful book has been shared. The gifts of the heart are also hers to share: a listening ear, a shoulder to cry on, a new insight, an encouraging touch. I can testify, with gratitude, to the impact retired officers have made on my life.

PRAYER

Killinger tells a story about a boy and an old man sitting on a dock in the late afternoon, fishing: 'They talked about many things – why sunsets are red, why the rain falls, why the seasons change, what life is like. Finally the boy looked up at the old man, as the old man was baiting his hook for him, and asked, "Does anybody ever see God?" "Son," said the old man, looking across the blue waters, "it's getting so I hardly see anything else."'

Retirement gives time for extended prayer, both intercessory prayer and personal, devotional prayer. It is a time for deepening, for discarding the extraneous and focusing more and more on Jesus.

HAVING IMPACT

While it may appear as though a retired officer loses the ability to have impact, it is clear in observing them that their opportunity for impact is much greater on a personal level following retirement. As an active officer with a pastor's heart and gifts, the struggle is how much energy we need to keep the big picture running, and how much time we can spend with individuals in counsel, prayer and community. With retirement, that balance shifts and the doors open for one-on-one discipleship and care. A friend of mine was approaching retirement, having served as a divisional leader for a number of years. When I asked her what she planned to do, she said: 'I want to be able to minister the grace of Christ to women. I don't know who, or where, or how, but that is the desire of my heart.'

LOOKING AHEAD IN HOPE

If what we have taught and preached through the years of officership has any bearing upon our lives we come to our final days with the glorious hope of Heaven. During my counselling internship I spent an afternoon with a gracious woman psychologist, Sara, who provided psychological services one day a week at a nursing home. As I watched her, I stood on holy ground as she spoke with a woman late in years about Heaven. Sara gently took her hand, read a few paragraphs from Joni Eareckson Tada's book *Heaven: Your Real Home* and spoke soothing words about what it meant to die and be in Heaven. She was able to ease the older woman's fears and awaken the hunger within her for Home.

It is at this time that we can draw upon the gift of image. I must admit that some of the classic images of Heaven are hard for me to grasp, such as the golden streets or angels sitting on clouds, playing harps. Two I find particularly helpful are shared by favourite authors.

First, Annie Lamott likens our coming Home to a child who's been dreadfully sick, spending a restless night alone in their bed. 'However, unknown to us, sometime during that long night our daddy has come to our room, lifted us in his arms, and brought us into our parent's bed – warm, comforting, safe, whole.'

The other is Dan Allender's image, sitting around a campfire with Jesus. Just as at those nights gathered around the campfire at retreats or staff devotions at camp, there is singing and a quieting of our hearts as we rest in the presence of our Saviour. In Allender's Heaven, Jesus turns to us with a welcoming smile, inviting us to tell our story. As we do, we see reflected in the light of the campfire those whose stories have intertwined with ours, who have shared our joy and sorrow, love and life. Allender's image is reminiscent of Charles Gabriel's verse:

> *Friends will be there I have loved long ago,*
> *Joy like a river around me will flow,*
> *Yet just a smile from my Saviour, I know,*
> *Will through the ages be glory for me.*

We can claim the promise of the apostle John's testimony: 'He will wipe every tear from their eyes. There will be no more death or mourning or crying or pain, for the old order of things has passed away ... Then the angel showed me the river of the water of life, as clear as crystal, flowing from the throne of God and of the Lamb ... The Spirit and the bride say, "Come!" And let him who hears say, "Come!" Whoever is thirsty, let him come; and whoever wished, let him take the free gift of the water of life' (Revelation 21:4; 22:1, 17 *TNIV*).

And so, in the end as at the beginning, the spiral returns to its origin, that of a journey of faith and courage. The springtime breezes have turned into the draughts and drifts of winter, yet they blow gently for the woman of strength who knows the sound of her Father's voice. And they bring with them the promise of a springtime that will stretch into eternity, the ultimate 'new birth'. So we wait, patiently, passionately, sometimes just holding onto our faith by a thread, because we know that 'the one who calls you is faithful and he will do it!' (1 Thessalonians 5:24 *TNIV*).

Resources

Adeney, Miriam. *A Time for Risking: Priorities for Women*. Multnomah, 1987.

Allender, Dan and Tremper Longman III. *Cry of the Soul: How Our Emotions Reveal Our Deepest Questions About God*. NavPress, 1994.

Allender, Dan and Tremper Longman III. *Intimate Allies*. Tyndale House Publishers, 1995.

Anderson, Lynn. *If I Really Believe, Why Do I Have These Doubts?* Bethany House Publishers, 1992.

Artress, Lauren. In Hancock, E. Lee and Lee Hancock, eds. *The Book of Women's Sermons: Hearing God in Each Other's Voices*. Riverhead Books, 1999.

Austin, Linda S. *What's Holding You Back? Eight Critical Choices for Women's Success*. Basic Books, 2000.

Barclay, William. *The Gospel of Luke,* revised edition. Westminster Press, 1975.

Barna, George. *The Future of the American Family*. Moody Press, 1993.

Ban Breathnach, Sarah. *Simple Abundance: A Daybook of Comfort and Joy*. Warner Books, 1995.

Booth, Catherine. *Female Ministry (1859)*. In *Terms of Empowerment: Salvation Army Women in Ministry*. The Salvation Army USA Eastern Territory, 2001.

Booth, Catherine Bramwell. *Catherine Booth*. Hodder and Stoughton, 1970.

Booth, Libbett. *Becoming Me. The Officer.*

Booth, William. Quoted in *The War Cry (USA)*, 23 October 1993.

Bringle, Mary Louise. *Soul Dye and Salt: Integrating Spiritual and Medical Understandings of Depression. The Journal of Pastoral Care*, 1996.

Brown Taylor, Barbara. *The Preaching Life*. Cowley Publications, 1993.

Brueggemann, Walter, quoted in *The Art of Spiritual Guidance*. Crossroads Publishing, 1992.

Buechner, Frederick. *Wishful Thinking*. Harper and Row, 1973.

Burrows, Eva, quoted by Gariepy, Henry. *General of God's Army: The Authorised Biography of General Eva Burrows*. Victor Books, 1993.

Campbell, Douglas F. *The Clergy Family in Canada: Focus on Adult PKs*. University of Toronto, Erindale College, 1995.

Chaves, Mark. *Ordaining Women: Culture and Conflict in Religious Organizations*. Harvard University Press, 1997.

Congo, Mary Guerrera. *The Truth Will Set You Free, But First It Will Make You Crazy*. In Gray, Elizabeth Dodson, ed. *Sacred Dimensions of Women's Experience*. Roundtable Press, 1988.

Crabb, Larry. *Inside Out*. NavPress, 1988.

205

Craik, Dinah Marie. *A Life for a Life*, 1859.

D'Arcy, Paula. *Gift of the Red Bird: A Spiritual Encounter*. Crossroads, 1996.

Dentiere, Marie. Quoted in Douglas, Jane Dempsey. *Reforming Women Interpret the Bible*. In Douglas, Jane Dempsey and James F. Kay, ed. *Women, Gender and Christian Community*. Westminster, 1997.

Detrick, Ralph L. and Mary Cline Detrick. *Marriages of Two Clergy-persons. Pastoral Psychology,* 1982.

Dobson, James. *Straight Talk: What Men Need to Know; What Women Should Understand*. Word Publishing, 1991.

Dobson, James. *Today's Christian Woman*, May/June 1988.

Duff, Nancy. *Vocation, Motherhood and Marriage*. In Douglas, Jane Dempsey and James F. Kay, ed. *Women, Gender and Christian Community*. Westminster, 1997

Dunlap, Susan J. *Counseling Depressed Women*. Westminster John Knox Press, 1991.

Erikson, Erik. *Identity and the Life Cycle*. Norton, 1980.

Fabry, Chris. *At the Corner of Mundane and Grace: Finding Glimpses of Glory in Ordinary Days*. WaterBrook Press, 1999.

Fischer, Kathleen. *From Darkness to Dawn: Spiritual Transformations at Midlife. Praying*, 1993.

Flagg, Deborah. *Softly Eclipsed. New Frontier*, 30 April 1997.

Fleming, Jean. *The Homesick Heart: Longing for Spiritual Intimacy*. NavPress, 1995.

Ford, Lucille. Interview. *North Central Business Journal*, January 2002.

Foster, Richard. *Celebration of Discipline: The Path to Spiritual Growth*. Harper and Row, 1978. *Prayer: Finding the Heart's True Home*. HarperSanFrancisco, 1992.

Frank, Jan. In Groom, Nancy. *Heart to Heart About Men: Words of Encouragement for Women of Integrity*. NavPress, 1995.

Fromm, Erich. *The Art of Loving*. Harper, 1956.

Fuchs, Esther, quoted in Bellis, Alice Ogden. *Helpmates, Harlots and Heroes*. Westminster/John Knox Press, 1994.

Gilligan, Carol. *In a Different Voice*. Harvard University Press, 1982.

Gire, Ken. *Windows of the Soul: Experiencing God in New Ways*. Zondervan, 1996.

Glasser, Connie and Barbara Steinberg Smalley. *Swim with the Dolphins: How Women Can Succeed in Corporate America on Their Own Terms*. Warner Books, 1995.

Goetz, David. *Is the Pastor's Family Safe at Home? Leadership*, XIII, 4. 1992.

International Commission on Officership: Final Report and the General's Consultation with Officers. The Salvation Army International Headquarters, 2000.

Gratton, Carolyn. *The Art of Spiritual Guidance*. Crossroads, 1992.

Greeley, Andrew. *Star Bright*. Forge Books, 2002.

Green, Roger. *Catherine Booth*. Baker Books, 1996.

Grimes, Emily May. *Speak, Lord, in the Stillness*, 1920.

Groeschal, Benedict. *Spiritual Passages: For Those Who See: The Psychology of Spiritual Development*. Crossroads, 1959.

Gudorf, Christine. Quoted in Miller-McLemore, Bonnie. *Also a Mother: Work and Family as Theological Dilemma*. Abingdon Press, 1994.

Hardesty, Nancy. *Women Called to Witness: Evangelical Feminism in the Nineteenth Century*. Abingdon Press, 1984.

Hart, Archibald. *Counseling the Depressed: Resources for Christian Counseling*. Word Publishing, 1987.

Hersh, Sharon. *The Desperation of God: A Reflection on the Feminine Desire for Relationship*. *Mars Hill Review*. 9. 1999, 27-38.

Hodder, Marjorie. *The War Cry* (USA), 23 October 1993.

Howatch, Susan. *Absolute Truths*. Alfred A. Knopf, 1995.

Hudson, Jackie. *Doubt, a Road to Growth*. Thomas Nelson, 1987.

Huggins, Kevin. *Parenting Adolescents*. NavPress, 1989. *Men and Women: Enjoying the Differences*. Zondervan, 1991.

Hunter, Brenda. *In the Company of Women: Deepening Our Relationship with the Important Women in Our Lives*. Multnomah, 1995. *The Power of Mother Love*. WaterBrook Press, 1998.

James, William. John McDermott, ed. *The Writings of William James: A Comprehensive Edition*. University of Chicago Press, 1978.

Jordan, Judith. *The Meaning of Mutuality*. Stone Center for Developmental Services and Studies, 1986.

Joseph, Jenny. *Warning*. In Hartz, Sandra Haldeman, ed. *When I Am an Old Woman I Shall Wear Purple*. Papier-Mache Press, 1987.

Josselson, Ruthellen. *Finding Herself: Pathways to Identity Development in Women*. Jossey-Bass, 1987.

Kidd, Sue Monk. *The Dance of the Dissident Daughter*. HarperSanFrancisco, 1996. *Example. Pastoral Psychology*. 1989.

Kieren, Dianne K. and Brenda Munro. *Handling Greedy Clergy Roles: A Dual Clergy Example. Pastoral Pyschology*. 1989.

Killinger, John. *Christ in the Seasons of Ministry*. Word Books. 1983.

Kroeger, Catherine Clark and Richard Clark. *I Suffer Not a Woman: Rethinking I Timothy 2:11-15 in Light of Ancient Evidence*. Baker Book House, 1992.

Lakoff, Robin. Quoted in Douglas, Jane Dempsey and James F. Kay, ed. *Women, Gender and Christian Community*. Westminster, 1997.

Lamott, Anne. *All New People*. North Point Press, 1989. *Bird by Bird: Some Instructions on Writing and Life*. Random House, 1994.

Langberg, Diane. *AACC Newsletter*, June 2001.

Larsson, John. *Salvationist Theology and Ethics for the New Millennium*. Word and Deed, 2001.

Lawless, Elaine. In Kienzie, Beverly Mayne and Pamela J. Walker, eds. *Women Preachers and Prophets through Two Millennia of Christianity*. University of California Press, 1998.

Lee, D. John, ed. *Storying Ourselves: A Narrative Perspective on Christians in Psychology*. Baker Books, 1993.

Lewis, C. S. *The Four Loves*. Harcourt, 1960.

Lindberg, Ingrid. *A Conversation with Colonel Ingrid Lindberg. Youth Department Newsletter*, USA Eastern Territory, 1980.

Lindbergh, Anne Morrow. *Gift from the Sea*. Random House, 1955.

Luhrs, Janet. *The Simple Living Guide*. Broadway Books, 1997.

Mains, David and Mains, Karen Burton. *Living, Loving, Leading: Creating a Home that Encourages Spiritual Growth*. Multnomah Press, 1988. *Open Heart, Open Home*. David C. Cook Publishers, 1976.

Mason, Mike. *The Mystery of Marriage: As Iron Sharpens Iron*. Multnomah Press, 1985.

Metz, Barbara and John Burchill. *The Enneagram and Prayer*. Dimension Books, 1987.

Miller, Jean Baker. *Toward a New Psychology of Women*. Beacon Press, 1977.

Miller-McLemore, Bonnie. *Also a Mother: Work and Family as Theological Dilemma*. Abingdon Press, 1994.

Milne, A.A. *House at Pooh Corner*. Methuen and Company, 1928.

Muto, Susan. *John of the Cross for Today: The Dark Night of the Soul*. Ave Maria Press, 1994.

Niebuhr, Reinhold. *Leaves from the Notebook of Tamed Cynic*. Willett, Clark and Colby, 1929.

Noren, Carol Marie. *The Woman in the Pulpit*. Abingdon Press, 1991.

Nouwen, Henri. *The Way of the Heart: Desert Spirituality and Contemplative Ministry*. Seabury Press, 1981. *Here and Now: Living in the Spirit*. Crossroads, 2002.

Paterson, Evangeline. *A Wish for My Children*. In *Seasons of Life: A Poetic Anthology*. Prometheus Books, 2000.

Percy, Walker. *The Second Coming*. Farrar, Straus, Giroux, 1980.

Peterson, Eugene. *The Wisdom of Each Other: A Conversation Between Spiritual Friends*. Zondervan, 1998.

Phillips, Michael. *Fatal Reaction: Antidotes to PK Poisoning. Leadership*. XIII. 4, 1992.

Quinn, Brian P. *The Depression Sourcebook*. Lowell House, 1997.

Rader, June. *A Conversation with Colonel Ingrid Lindberg. Youth Department Newsletter*, USA Eastern Territory, 1980.

Rader, Kay. *Keeping the Dream Alive*. In *Terms of Empowerment: Salvation Army Women in Ministry*. The Salvation Army USA Eastern Territory, 2001.

Rallings, E.M. and David J.Pratto. *Two-clergy Marriages: A Special Case of Dual Careers*. University Press of America, 1984.

Rayburn, Carole A, Lee J. Richmond, and Lynn Rogers. *Religious Professionals and Clergy Spouses: Stress Among Religious Leaders. Journal of Pastoral Counseling*. 23, 1988.

Rinehart, Stacy. *Upside Down: The Paradox of Servant Leadership*. NavPress, 1998.

Rohr, Richard. *Everything Belongs: The Gift of Contemplative Prayer*. Crossroad Publishing, 1999. *Hope Against Darkness: The Transforming Vision of Saint Francis in an Age of Anxiety*. St Anthony Messenger Press, 2001.

Rupp, Joyce. *Praying Our Good-byes*. Ave Maria Press, 1988. *Dear Heart, Come Home: The Path of Midlife Spirituality*. Crossroad Publishing, 1997

Ryan, Geoff. *First Family*. *Horizons*, September/October, 2001.

Sarton, May. *Mrs Stevens Hears the Mermaids Sing*. W. W. Norton, 1965.

Saunders, Sue. *Married Couples in Clergy Partnerships: Opportunities and Problems. Evangelical Review of Theology*. 1991.

Senter, Ruth. *The Seasons of Friendship: A Search for Intimacy*. Zondervan, 1989. *Longing for Love: Conversations with a Compassionate Heavenly Father*. NavPress, 1991.

Shaw, Luci. *God in the Dark: Through Grief and Beyond*. Zondervan, 1993.

Smedes, Lewis. *Caring and Commitment: Learning to Live the Love We Promise*. Harper and Row, 1988.

Spencer, Aida Besancon. *Beyond the Curse: Women Called to Ministry*. Thomas Nelson, 1985.

Sweet, Leonard. *Soul Tsunami*. Zondervan, 1999.

Tada, Joni Eareckson. *Heaven: Your Real Home*. Zondervan, 1997.

Tan, Siang-Yang and John Ortberg Jr. *Understanding Depression: Strategic Pastoral Counseling Resources*. Baker Books, 1995.

Terry, James W., Absence and Presence, in Hagen, June Steffensen, ed. *Gender Matters: Women's Studies for the Christian Community*. Academie Books, 1990.

The Cloud of Unknowing. www.ccel.org/u/unknowing/cloud.htm.

Tisdale, Leonora Tubbs. *Women's Ways of Communicating: A New Blessing for Preaching*. In Douglas, Jane Dempsey and James F. Kay, ed. *Women, Gender and Christian Community*. Westminster, 1997.

Townsend, John. *The Home Litmus Test. Leadership*. XII, 4;1992.

Trout, Margaret. *The General was a Lady: The Story of Evangeline Booth*. A. J. Holman, 1980.

Vanderlaan, Eunice. *Leadership*. XIII. 4; 1992.

Van Leeuwen, Mary Stewart. *Gender and Grace: Love, Work and Parenting in a Changing World*. Intervarsity Press, 1990.

VanVonderen, Jeff. *Families Where Grace is in Place*. Bethany House, 1992.

Wangarin, Walter. *Reliving the Passion: Meditations on the Suffering, Death and Resurrection of Jesus as Recorded in Mark*. Zondervan, 1992.

Watson, Wayne. *Come Home. The Way Home*. Word, 1998.

White, John. *Parents in Pain*. InterVarsity Press, 1979.

Williams, Margery. *The Velveteen Rabbit*. Knopf, 1985.

Worthington, Everett L. Jr. *Hope-focused Marriage Counseling: A Guide to Brief Therapy*. Intervarsity Press, 1999.